Queering Methodology

This groundbreaking collection explores the complexities of researching the lives of lesbian and queer women. It critically interrogates the concept of 'lesbian', especially as applied to research praxis. Who or what is a 'lesbian' and why does this category matter? How is research shaped by such categorisations and why? What does it mean for research that identities can be fluid and changing? Further, this collection examines social formation of power from an intersectional perspective in relation to lesbian and queer women's experiences, exploring complex tensions and inequalities in relation to class, race and trans identities for example. These chapters by world-renowned scholars bring together the compelling accounts of research dilemmas, ethics, sensitivities and nuances that will resonate for many researchers.

This book highlights how gender, sexuality and power intersect within and beyond the research project, illuminating how research can generate new questions as well as provide important insights.

The chapters in this book were originally published as a special issue of the *Journal of Lesbian Studies*.

Róisín Ryan-Flood is a Professor of Sociology and the Director of the Centre for Intimate and Sexual Citizenship at the University of Essex, UK. Her books include *Lesbian Motherhood: Gender, Families and Sexual Citizenship* (2009) and *Transnationalising Reproduction: Third Party Conception in a Globalised World* (Routledge, 2018). She is the co-editor of the journal *Sexualities*.

Alison Rooke is a writer and researcher. After a long association with Goldsmiths, University of London, UK, where she was Senior Lecturer, she became the Director of the social research company Art of Regeneration.

Queering Methodology
Lessons and Dilemmas from Lesbian Lives

Edited by
Róisín Ryan-Flood and Alison Rooke

LONDON AND NEW YORK

First published 2023
by Routledge
4 Park Square, Milton Park, Abingdon, Oxon, OX14 4RN

and by Routledge
605 Third Avenue, New York, NY 10158

Routledge is an imprint of the Taylor & Francis Group, an informa business

© 2023 Taylor & Francis

All rights reserved. No part of this book may be reprinted or reproduced or utilised in any form or by any electronic, mechanical, or other means, now known or hereafter invented, including photocopying and recording, or in any information storage or retrieval system, without permission in writing from the publishers.

Trademark notice: Product or corporate names may be trademarks or registered trademarks, and are used only for identification and explanation without intent to infringe.

British Library Cataloguing-in-Publication Data
A catalogue record for this book is available from the British Library

ISBN13: 978-1-032-29872-6 (hbk)
ISBN13: 978-1-032-29874-0 (pbk)
ISBN13: 978-1-003-30246-9 (ebk)

DOI: 10.4324/9781003302469

Typeset in Garamond
by codeMantra

Publisher's Note
The publisher accepts responsibility for any inconsistencies that may have arisen during the conversion of this book from journal articles to book chapters, namely the inclusion of journal terminology.

Disclaimer
Every effort has been made to contact copyright holders for their permission to reprint material in this book. The publishers would be grateful to hear from any copyright holder who is not here acknowledged and will undertake to rectify any errors or omissions in future editions of this book.

Contents

	Citation Information	vi
	Notes on Contributors	viii
1	Introduction *Róisín Ryan-Flood and Alison Rooke*	1
2	The Re-Making of Sexual Kinds: Queer Subjects and the Limits of Representation *Lisa Blackman*	8
3	The Lady Vanishes: On Never Knowing, Quite, Who Is a Lesbian *Kath Weston*	22
4	Queer in the Field: On Emotions, Temporality, and Performativity in Ethnography *Alison Rooke*	34
5	Researching Domestic Violence in Same-Sex Relationships—A Feminist Epistemological Approach to Survey Development *Marianne Hester and Catherine Donovan*	46
6	Producing Cosmopolitan Sexual Citizens on *The L Word* *Kellie Burns and Cristyn Davies*	59
7	Complexities and Complications: Intersections of Class and Sexuality *Yvette Taylor*	74
8	Researching "Race" in Lesbian Space: A Critical Reflection *Nina Held*	88
9	Queering Representation: Ethics and Visibility in Research *Róisín Ryan-Flood*	100
	Index	113

Citation Information

The chapters in this book were originally published in the *Journal of Lesbian Studies*, volume 13, issue 2 (2009). When citing this material, please use the original page numbering for each article as follows:

Chapter 1
Que(e)rying Methodology: Lessons and Dilemmas from Lesbian Lives: An Introduction
Róisín Ryan-Flood and Alison Rooke
Journal of Lesbian Studies, volume 13, issue 2 (2009) pp. 115–121

Chapter 2
The Re-Making of Sexual Kinds: Queer Subjects and the Limits of Representation
Lisa Blackman
Journal of Lesbian Studies, volume 13, issue 2 (2009) pp. 122–135

Chapter 3
The Lady Vanishes: On Never Knowing, Quite, Who Is a Lesbian
Kath Weston
Journal of Lesbian Studies, volume 13, issue 2 (2009) pp. 136–148

Chapter 4
Queer in the Field: On Emotions, Temporality, and Performativity in Ethnography
Alison Rooke
Journal of Lesbian Studies, volume 13, issue 2 (2009) pp. 149–160

Chapter 5
Researching Domestic Violence in Same-Sex Relationships—A Feminist Epistemological Approach to Survey Development
Marianne Hester and Catherine Donovan
Journal of Lesbian Studies, volume 13, issue 2 (2009) pp. 161–173

Chapter 6
Producing Cosmopolitan Sexual Citizens on The L Word
Kellie Burns and Cristyn Davies
Journal of Lesbian Studies, volume 13, issue 2 (2009) pp. 174–188

Chapter 7

Complexities and Complications: Intersections of Class and Sexuality
Yvette Taylor
Journal of Lesbian Studies, volume 13, issue 2 (2009) pp. 189–203

Chapter 8

Researching "Race" in Lesbian Space: A Critical Reflection
Nina Held
Journal of Lesbian Studies, volume 13, issue 2 (2009) pp. 204–215

Chapter 9

Queering Representation: Ethics and Visibility in Research
Róisín Ryan-Flood
Journal of Lesbian Studies, volume 13, issue 2 (2009) pp. 216–228

For any permission-related enquiries please visit:
http://www.tandfonline.com/page/help/permissions

Notes on Contributors

Lisa Blackman is based at Goldsmiths and works at the intersection of body studies, media psychology, and media and cultural theory. Her research focuses upon the broad areas of affect, subjectivity, the body and embodiment. She also has a keen interest in mental health research and activism and was one of the early pioneers of the Hearing Voices Movement. She has published six books across these areas, including *Immaterial Bodies: Affect, Embodiment, Mediation* (2012); *Haunted Data: Affect, Transmedia, Weird Science* (2019); and *The Body: The Key Concepts* (2021, Routledge, second edition). She is currently completing a book *Abuse Assemblages: Emotions and Affects of Convolution*. She has been a member of the Centre for Feminist Research at Goldsmiths since its inception and has been Co-Director since 2016. She was the Principal Investigator on a British Academy-funded project 'Cultures of Consent: Examining the Complexity of Sexual Misconduct and Power within Universities' with Dr Yasmin Gunaratnam (Co-Investigator) and Chloe Turner (Research Assistant). https://www.gold.ac.uk/media-communications/staff/blackman/

Kellie Burns is Senior Lecturer in the School of Education and Social Work at The University of Sydney, Australia. Her research is historical and sociological, exploring the intersections of gender, sexuality, health and schooling. Her forthcoming edited book, entitled *Curriculum of the Body and the School as Clinic*, examines the school as a site for the management of childhood health and children's bodily norms.

Cristyn Davies is Research Fellow in the Specialty of Child and Adolescent Health in the Faculty of Medicine and Health at the University of Sydney Clinical School at Children's Hospital Westmead, and is a researcher on the Wellbeing, Health and Youth NHMRC Centre of Research Excellence in Adolescent Health. She is also Co-Chair of the Human Rights Council of Australia and is an ambassador for Twenty10 Incorporating the Gay and Lesbian Counselling Service NSW. She has expertise in gender and sexuality; child and adolescent health; vaccination; sexual and reproductive health; health education and comprehensive sexuality education; media and communications; and knowledge translation and implementation science. She has published widely in the areas of her expertise, including co-authoring *Mediating Sexual Citizenship: Neoliberal Subjectivities in Television Culture*, Routledge (2018).

Catherine Donovan is Professor of Sociology and the Head of Department at Durham University, UK, where she is a member of the Centre for Research into Violence and

Abuse (CRiVA). She has conducted research into the family and intimate lives of lesbians, gay men, bisexual and, more recently, transgender women and men and non-binary gendered folk for over 20 years. For the last 15 of those years, she has been researching domestic and sexual violence and abuse and, latterly, hate crime. In addition, her work involves research on changing the culture that supports violence and abuse with active bystanders and universities' responses to concerns about gender-based violence.

Nina Held is Lecturer in Social Policy at the University of Salford, UK. Her research interests are situated within the areas of LGBTQI+ asylum and human rights, gender and sexuality studies, critical 'race' scholarship and sexual and emotional geographies. From 2016 to 2021 she was Lecturer in Sociology as well as Postdoctoral Research Fellow in Law at the University of Sussex, UK, where she was leading the German case study of the ERC-funded project *SOGICA – Sexual Orientation and Gender Identity Claims of Asylum: A Human Rights Challenge (2016-2020)*. Before returning to academia in 2016, she worked for different NGOs in Manchester, such as Trafford Rape Crisis, Freedom from Torture and the Lesbian Immigration Support Group. She has published widely and is a co-founder of the Queer European Asylum Network (QUEAN).

Marianne Hester is Professor at the University of Bristol, UK, where she is the Chair in Gender, Violence and International Policy in the School for Policy Studies. She is an Editor in Chief of the *Journal of Gender-Based Violence*. She has conducted research into many aspects of gender-based violence, including studies into the extent and nature, service use and service need of lesbian, gay male, bisexual and transgendered victims/survivors of domestic and sexual violence. Recent work has explored the meaning of 'justice' for victims-survivors and measurement of domestic abuse in national crime surveys, including voices from LGBT+ communities.

Alison Rooke is a sociologist with a specialism in urban theory and creative research methods and has published widely in these fields. She has an on-going interest in the dynamics of participation in the city brought about through arts-led interventions, urban policy and regeneration. She has a long history of working collaboratively with local communities, activists and cross-sectoral stakeholders in educational and community settings on a national and European scale. Over many years, she has worked in partnership with arts, cultural and educational institutions developing critical and collaborative approaches to research and evaluation at a local, national and international level. These projects have focused on the areas of urban regeneration and governance, third sector research, active citizenship, participatory urban planning and social arts practice. She is the Director of the not-for-profit research consultancy Art of Regeneration Ltd.

Róisín Ryan-Flood is Professor of Sociology and the Director of the Centre for Intimate and Sexual Citizenship (CISC) at the University of Essex, UK. Her research interests are gender, sexuality, kinship, digital intimacies and feminist epistemology. She is the author of *Lesbian Motherhood: Gender, Sexuality and Citizenship* (2009), and the co-editor of *Secrecy and Silence in the Research Process* (Routledge, 2010) and *Transnationalising Reproduction* (Routledge, 2018). She is also the co-editor of the journal *Sexualities: Studies in Culture and Society*.

Yvette Taylor is Professor in the School of Education at the University of Strathclyde, UK, and has published four sole-authored books based on funded research: *Working-class Lesbian Life* (2007); *Lesbian and Gay Parenting* (2009); *Fitting into Place? Class and Gender Geographies and Temporalities* (2012) and *Making Space for Queer Identifying Religious Youth (2015)*. She has recently co-authored *Feminist Repetitions in Higher Education: Interrupting Career Categories* (2020) and is working on a new book *Working-Class Queers* (2022). Edited titles include *Educational Diversity* (2012), *The Entrepreneurial University* (2014), *Feeling Academic in the Neoliberal University* (2018) and *The Palgrave Handbook of Imposter Syndrome in Higher Education* (2022). She co-edits the *Routledge Advances in Critical Diversities Series*.

Kath Weston is British Academy Global Professor at the University of Edinburgh, UK, and Professor of Anthropology at the University of Virginia, Charlottesville, USA. Her recent work focuses on embodiment and visceral engagement, integrating material from kinship studies, social studies of finance, political ecology and science and technology studies. She has received multiple honors and awards, including the British Academy Global Professorship, a Guggenheim Fellowship, National Science Foundation grants, visiting professorships at Tokyo University and the University of Cambridge and two Ruth Benedict Book Prizes. Her books include *Families We Choose: Lesbians, Gays, Kinship*; *Traveling Light: On the Road with America's Poor*; and *Animate Planet: Making Visceral Sense of Living in a High-Tech Ecologically Damaged World.*

Introduction

RÓISÍN RYAN-FLOOD

ALISON ROOKE

Questions of ethics, accountability, and representation have long animated the social sciences. Feminist writing has played a key role in highlighting the significance of power relations at all points in the research process. The personal identities of the researcher and researched are understood to affect the knowledge produced. Thus, the situatedness of the researcher and participants influence how they interact, the empirical data produced, and the epistemological terrain within which it is interpreted (Oakley, 1981; Ramazanoglu and Holland, 2002). The identities of the researcher and respondents are understood as plural and addressed in relation to gender, race, sexuality, class, age, and other axes of belonging. It is acknowledged that differences in identity can also constitute differences in power (Letherby, 2003). In short, the research process is not an objective, clean business but rather is riven with power relations and is often a messy, complex interplay of subjectivities, identities, and emotions (Fonow and Cook, 1991; Maynard and Purvis, 1994; Stanley, 1997). Rather than viewing these complexities as a shortcoming of the research process, using reflexivity and other analytical tools allows the researcher to reflect upon the dilemmas and challenges of research. This process helps to illuminate wider social relations and modes of intersubjectivity.

Social and cultural research on lesbian lives can present particular challenges. Work on sexuality and intimate life requires navigating sensitive issues. Writing about minority groups brings certain expectations and responsibilities. The researcher may grapple with exposing the lives of a vulnerable group to a hegemonic audience who may be unfamiliar with or unsympathetic to their difficulties. There may be more immediately pressing problems with recruitment—minority groups may not be highly motivated to participate in research, for a variety of reasons. They may feel uncomfortable exposing their lives to a researcher or they may feel over researched and scrutinized. Any social group may find it difficult to make time to participate in research. Research on people living outside of heterosexuality can present difficulties of definition—Who is a "lesbian"? As queer theory has illustrated, sexual identities are fluid and mutable. Sexual practices may not conform to conventional understandings of identity categories. Writing about a minority group can also present dilemmas in writing up—how to represent this group in ways that are sensitive to the wider homophobic context in which their lives are lived.

These are among the dilemmas touched on in this special issue. Each contribution to the special issue represents a contribution to wider debates about how to theorize and interpret the practice of research on lesbian lifestyles. Some of these articles were presented at a panel at the Lesbian Lives conference held at University College Dublin in 2007. Others were a response to a subsequent call for papers. All contributors were invited to reflect upon the experience of researching lesbian lives. The fascinating series of articles that were submitted reveal that this remains a lively and vital field of work. The aim of this special issue is to map out some of the challenges, shifts, and transformations that characterize work in the field of lesbian studies but that speak to broader methodological debates across a range of interdisciplinary sites. Each of the eight following articles explores different facets of intersections of sexuality, subjectivity, and identity within contemporary contexts. A number of themes emerge from the articles. The oftentimes intangibility of the term "lesbian" presents particular challenges for researchers. Issues of diversity, difference, and representation also emerge as key issues for work in this field.

The interrogations of the epistemological, ontological, and ethical issues exemplified by these articles have significance beyond a consideration of methodological dimensions of making sense of lesbian lives. The articles in this issue are also potentially useful to sociological and cultural theorists working across a number of sites and disciplines and to the questions facing theorists concerned with identities, difference, and power, their contemporary articulations and manifestations. The articles here are concerned with the ways in which people both live with and make sense of the meanings of identity categories and the "multiple contradictory interpellations of social subjects" (Fraser, 1998: 149) in an ever changing neoliberal cultural landscape. Many of the articles explore the dangers of the reification of sociological categories such as "race," "sexuality," "class," or "researcher" and the ways that they seductively become the substance of research rather than the processes by which these subjectivities come to make sense. They are also instructive for researchers and writers working across a range of disciplines who are researching "sensitive issues" and those individuals and communities who are often described as "vulnerable" or "hard to reach."

In the first article, "The Re-making of Sexual Kinds: Queer Subjects and the Limits of Representation," Lisa Blackman offers an insightful methodological framework for understanding the ways in which lesbians and gay men feature in the contemporary sociocultural landscape and the articulation of the relationships between specific sexed subject-positions and the cultural logics they enact and perform. Blackman's engaging and complex argument offers ways of foregrounding queer and heterosexual subjectivities as a methodological concern. This is a welcome contribution in a moment when sexual identities such as lesbian, ostensibly based on fixed difference, appear to be contested as identities become increasingly governed by an ethics of choice. Blackman interrogates the trope of flexibility and the figure of the post-gay and heteroflexible subject to show how lesbian and gay cultures that are considered socially marginal are symbolically significant to proximate straightness. Blackman's insightful analysis of the logics of heteroflexibility show clearly why theorists need to pay more attention to the dilemmas and contradictions that face lesbian, gay, bisexual, and transgender (LGBT) subjects as we negotiate how we have come to be known, in relation to the exigencies of our diverse lives and lifestyles.

In the next article, "The Lady Vanishes: On Never Knowing, Quite, Who Is a Lesbian," Kath Weston also highlights some of the difficulties in defining "the lesbian." What may to many seem like an initially self-evident category has of course been long understood by theorists of sexuality to encompass complex processes of belonging, the possibility of flexible desires and sexual histories, as well as individual and social acknowledgment. Rather than providing a coherent definition for a lesbian, or lamenting the difficulty of categorization, Weston argues in favor of a reconsideration of the notion of the limit itself. Instead of viewing the limit as a lack, Weston suggests that we consider the potential of the limit for providing new insights. It is the moment of "vanishing" in the search for certainties that illuminates assumptions and uncertainties. Thus, the slipperiness of sexual categories suggests the flexibility of all sexual identities.

Alison Rooke's article, "Queer in the Field: On Emotions, Temporality, and Performativity in Ethnography," explores the possibility of queering ethnography. This article is a reflection on a year of ethnographic fieldwork conducted in relation to a lesbian and gay community center in London. The research was concerned with the ways in which working-class lesbian and bisexual women experience the meanings of their sexual identities on an everyday basis. Rooke explores the epistemological, ontological, and ethical dimensions of ethnographic research into lesbian and bisexual women's lives, arguing that queer ethnography is not merely ethnography that focuses on researching queer lives, but that it is also a matter of taking queer theory seriously in order to question the conventions of ethnographic research. These conventions include the stability and coherence of the ethnographic self, and performativity of the ethnographic self in writing and doing research. To queer ethnography then, is to bend the established orientation of ethnography in its method, ethics, and reflexive philosophical principles while simultaneously attempting to do justice to the ways in which informants live the categories. Her article is concerned with the degree of complexity that is often erased in the straightforward use of the terms "lesbian" or "bisexual."

Continuing the theme of the problematics of categorizing sexualities and the pragmatics of conducting empirical work that employs them, Marianne Hester and Catherine Donovan explore the challenges of survey research with LGBT communities. Their article, "Researching Domestic Violence in Same-Sex Relationships—A Feminist Epistemological Approach to Survey Development," draws on recently completed research by the authors, involving a detailed study of love and domestic violence in same-sex and heterosexual relationships. This is the hitherto most detailed study of its kind in the United Kingdom. Empirical work in the quantitative tradition remains important in providing invaluable information about LGBT lives, which are often excluded entirely or incompletely incorporated into wider surveys. The research findings suggest distinct patterns of violence in gay and lesbian relationships. Employing feminist and discursive approaches to this methodology prompts interesting discussion of the issues raised. The researchers were rooted in understandings of experiences of domestic violence, including experiences and intersections related to gender and sexuality. This allowed development of a detailed survey approach that takes into account a range of abusive behaviors as well as impact, context, and abuse of partners in intimate relationships. The article frames the research in terms of "how we know" about violence in same-sex relationships and heterosexual relationships and the ways that research on the experience of domestic violence tells us about the features and dynamics of abuse while allowing new knowledge to emerge. The approach thus takes us a step further in analysis of domestic violence by moving beyond the generally heteronormative approaches of most surveys while also taking into account lesbian, let alone gay male and heterosexual, positionings and specificities.

Issues of representation also emerge in the article by Kellie Burns and Cristyn Davies, "Producing Cosmopolitan Sexual Citizens on *The L Word*," which explores the relationship between neo-liberalism, cosmopolitanism, and sexual citizenship. Their analysis draws on the television program *The L Word*, a show that depicts the lives of a group of lesbian characters in contemporary Los Angeles. In the article, they highlight the ways in which lesbian subjectivities are produced within a wider context of neo-liberalism and consumption in visual culture. They explore the significance of a cultural landmark such as *The L Word* for an understanding of what lesbian television as a site of cultural production *does*: what it produces, consumes, normalizes, and curtails. However, the article avoids the quantification approach of who is included or excluded from this realm of representation. Rather, the authors acknowledge the absences, but attempt to consider what possibilities and constraints these images and related subtexts offer for the shaping of contemporary queer subjectivities. The article makes a number of important points about the racialization, commodification, and fetishization of lesbian otherness.

The next two articles interrogate the intersections of class, gender, sexuality, and race in sociological research. Yvette Taylor's article, "Complexities and Complications: Intersections of Class and Sexuality," foregrounds the importance of class to the analysis of sexualities. Rather than merely rehearsing theoretical debates, Taylor draws on extensive empirical data that was gathered by conducting interviews with 53 interviewees who considered themselves to be working class and lesbian, to illuminate the tension between the theoretical complexities of intersectionality and the research appliance of this. Here Taylor shows how classed and sexual identities are felt with contradictory emotions being both positive choices and positions that can be grounds for discrimination and silence. The "complexities and complications" of a project concerned with class, gender, and sexuality as coherent lived experiences are interrogated here. Taylor also considers the significance of the lesbian researcher's classed subjectivity, which has been passed over when foregrounding the commonalities of sexuality in discussions about access to "informants" and the ongoing navigation of sameness and difference in the research process.

Nina Held's article, "Researching 'Race' in Lesbian Space: A Critical Reflection," also examines intersubjective dimensions of ethnographic research through a reflexive consideration of the embodied politics of researching race in lesbian bars. Like Taylor, Held moves on from a theoretical discussion of the researcher's gendered, classed, and racialized positionality and its impact on the research process and the data produced, to explore how "race" is actually *made* in/through the research. By drawing on one year of ethnographic fieldwork in two lesbian bars in the North West of England, this article shows how "race," in particular Whiteness, was constructed through participant observation in the ethnographic field. Held uses her field notes with honesty and reflexivity to interrogate her own racialized ways of seeing and sensing the field as a White woman. This article includes a plea for the development of the social researcher's consciousness and against simplistic use of racial categories in the often unspoken process of "race making" when doing research on lesbian lives where "race" is not the primary matter.

The final article in this collection, by Róisín Ryan-Flood—titled "Queering Representation: Ethics and Visibility in Research"—considers some of the ethical dilemmas encountered in the research, writing, and dissemination of work on lesbian lives. In particular, it addresses the tension between the researcher's need to tell women's stories while negotiating considerations of their vulnerability in homophobic contexts. Ryan-Flood draws on extensive research with lesbian parents in two European countries, Sweden and Ireland. The impact of strategies of openness and invisibility in each of these national contexts are considered in relation to their epistemological implications during the recruitment of participants and the process of data collection and analysis. The ethical dilemmas encountered challenge conceptualizations of "the field" as a spatially bounded entity. Rather, it is the nature of political standpoints and community belonging that relationships and events influencing "the field" continue to evolve long after a period spent in a particular geographical location is concluded. By thus politically situating "the field," it becomes clear why issues of representation and ethics can be central to the research process. Ryan-Flood also sets out the dilemmas facing those of us who research lesbian lives in an academic environment that encourages the researcher's engagement in public worlds of the academy, political debate, and the media. The desire to effect change here is tempered by the knowledge that one's often nuanced arguments and sensitive renderings of our informants' lives may well be distorted in the glare of public scrutiny.

All of the articles in this special issue explore the complex links between identity, subjectivity, sexuality, intertextuality, representation, and ethics. In the context of shifting boundaries for sexual citizenship, it remains important to trace these interconnections within the research process. In their analyses of power relations, multiple identities, heteronormativity, intimacy, and ethical concerns, the authors provide a range of insights to bear on debates about researching lesbian lives. The rich empirical material that they draw on highlights contemporary contexts for work in this area. The articles are also salient for wider discussions of representation, ethics, and intimate citizenship. This special issue provides a brief foray into the range of debates and developments in this fascinating field. Hopefully, the work here also opens up new questions and insights for further debate and research.

REFERENCES

Fraser, N. "Heterosexism, Misrecognition and Capitalism: A Response to Judith Butler," *New Left Review, 228*, 1998: 140–50.

Fonow, M., and J. A. Cook, eds. *Beyond Methodology: Feminist Scholarship as Lived Research*. Bloomington: Indiana University Press, 1991.

Letherby, G. *Feminist Research in Theory and Practice*. Buckingham, Open University Press, 2003.

Maynard, M. and J. Purvis. *Researching Women's Lives from a Feminist Perspective*. London: Taylor & Francis, 1994.

Oakley, A. "Interviewing Women: A Contradiction in Terms?" In H. Roberts, ed., *Doing Feminist Research*. London: Routledge, 1981: 30–61.

Ramazanoglu, C. and J. Holland. *Feminist Methodology: Challenges and Choices*. London, Sage, 2002.

Stanley, L. *Knowing Feminisms*. London: Sage, 1997.

The Re-Making of Sexual Kinds: Queer Subjects and the Limits of Representation

LISA BLACKMAN

This article discusses the importance of re-inventing subjectivity as an important analytic concern for understanding the production of lesbian sexualities. It explores the problems and possibilities with focusing on representational practices, and extends such work by analyzing the complex dilemmas, cultural logics, anxieties, and silences that are performed and enacted, particularly in the context of the hetero/lesbian. It argues that the psychosocial dimensions of representational practices might be usefully engaged by focusing on the "dialogic unconscious" that produces the negated background context of such practices. This is discussed in relation to the neo-liberal cultural logic of choice, and the distinction between flexible and rigid bodies.

INTRODUCTION

This special issue offers an interesting context to venture some methodological comments on the enduring question of how best to approach, study, represent, and even change the orthodox ways in which lesbian sexualities have come into being as particular kinds of (research) objects. Working as a critical psychologist throughout the eighties and nineties, the study of representation-as-signification and its relationship to the regulation of sexualities was a key methodological focus (Blackman and Walkerdine, 2001). The focus on representation-as-signification allowed an exploration of the categories and concepts that become available for self-definition, identification, and invention of personhood(s). The examination of those sexed "subject-positions" produced across mainstream film, television, magazine culture, advertising and marketing, and so forth, has produced a cartography of normalization, where the sexual Other has been analyzed for the symbolically central role they play in confirming heterosexuality as normal and natural. This focus on the *stereotype* as productive of sexed norms has also allowed a focus on how stereotypes could be both ambivalent and contradictory (Bhabha, 1994). The sexual Other could be an object of derision, hatred, scorn, and humiliation as well as the site of more desirous and erotic fantasies and desires. The important focus of this approach to representational practices is the importance given over to the complex psychic structures, or "structures of feeling" (Williams, 1977), which produce a range of investments and identifications that are primarily somatic, affective, non-cognitive, and non-conscious. In other words, the psychic investments are not rational and self-calculating but operate in a realm that is felt and not necessarily easily available for articulation. This raises important questions about how to examine and investigate the relationships between representational practices and subjectivities and foregrounds the important issues of embodiment, investment, and the affective in our relational connections (see Hemmings, 2005).

The issue I want to consider in this article is the extent to which the psychosocial dimensions of representational practices might be augmented by considering work within critical psychology that attends to the conflicts, dilemmas, and "dialogic unconscious" (Billig, 1997), which articulate the relationships between sexed subject-positions and the cultural logics they enact and perform. This will direct our attention to the complex question of how subjectivities are produced at the intersection of a relational matrix, which might include desire, imagination, affect, emotion, power, discourse, and signification.[1] The re-focusing on subjectivity as a methodological concern is important in moving beyond the binary structuring of ambivalence that we find in work on the colonial stereotype, for example, to explore the multiplication of dilemmas that are articulated across and between the plurality of differently sexed subject positions. It would seem that in the current context the re-prioritization of subjectivity as an important analytic and methodological concern is all the more imperative given the emergence of new forms of queer subjectivities. These include transgendered subjects who challenge both gendered and sexed forms of heteronormativity (Halberstam, 1998; Prosser, 1998), a range of new cultural practices associated with queer youth culture (Driver, 2008), post-feminism (Gill, 2006; McRobbie, 2005), and the shift across the humanities away from representation to exploring the production of affect as a key ontological and epistemological focus (Clough, 2007; Hemmings, 2005).

HETEROFLEXIBLE: A BREAK FROM ROUTINE

One of the problems of remaining at the level of representation in our methodologies is how to understand the significance and salience of new sexed subject positions that present sexuality as unfixed, fluid, temporary, or even with the category of "post-gay" remove sexual identity from sexual preference altogether. The apparent un-fixing of different sexualities as maligned Others and the increasing fluidity of (sexual) lifestyles inaugurates a re-making of sexual kinds. What we might see if we remain at the level of representation is a homosexualization of popular culture, or even the heterosexualization of different sexualities, such that the vexed question of how to understand this un-fixing remains fraught with difficulties. This has already been played out in debates and discussions within post-feminism that started with positive declarations and statements by some feminist academics, which have been tempered in more recent writings by a focus on the cultural production of psychopathology and its link to (post-feminist) female rage, melancholia, and depression (Blackman, 2004, 2006; Gil, 2006; McRobbie, 2005; Walkerdine, Lucey, and Melody, 2001). The question of psychopathology is an important one for lesbian methodologies to address, and even more so at a time when, for many, the reference to a psychological realm (that is understood relationally and discursively) is viewed as "bad theory,"[2] or as an unhealthy and obsessive focus on pain and misery ignoring our possible joyful becomings (Braidotti, 2002, 2006). The pendulum-like swing from regulation to resistance, fixity to fluidity, and identity to becoming discloses the paradoxes of subjectivity that this article hopes to make visible, and to offer some methodological comments as to where we might go.

I want to start by taking the figure of the *heteroflexible* as a condensed image of some of the problems that we face in re-focusing our attention on the question of subjectivities. As many scholars have argued there appear to be a diverse range of new subject positions open to the queer and straight consumer alike, which claim through one's own choice, freedom, and agency to expand one's experience of personhood. These include the metrosexual, the "post-gay," the *heteroflexible*, the midriff, and the yummy mummy (Gill, 2006). Sean Nixon (2001), Frank Mort (1987), and Ken Plummer (2001) have all shown how in the field of consumption, style, and fashion, the borders between straight and gayness have blurred. What I want to focus on here is how the *heteroflexible* develops this logic by seeming to expand heterosexuality, while locating queer subjects within the psychologically inferior realm of habit and routine. The *heteroflexible* as an iconic image embodies an invitation to straight men and women to open themselves to the possibility of emotional and sexual same-sex relationships. This might include taking style tips and advice from mainstream lesbian and gay culture (cf. Blackman, in press), but usually involves some commitment to "trying it out."

This both/and rather than either/or opposition, particularly of lesbianism to feminine heterosexuality, marks the heterosexual woman who embraces a lesbian identity as a temporary interruption to the solid and indomitable march of heterosexual desire. I will argue that the concepts that govern these cultural logics need to be understood and analyzed by considering what kinds of dilemmas currently govern heterosexual relationships. I will consider this problematic by focusing on the "hetero/lesbian" as opposed to the gay man although my discussion has repercussions for the broader dialogic context that might govern these representations (see Blackman 2004, 2006). What I will argue is that the re-making of sexual kinds made possible or probable by these representations does not simply present evidence of a "heterosexualization" of different sexualities. Rather, this logic of movement and expansion enacts or performs cultural norms that present the normative subject as one exercising choice, freedom, and autonomy. This represents an un-fixing and re-fixing of sexual kinds through marking out bodies according to distinctions made between the flexible and the rigid. This argument adds further weight to Gayle Rubin's argument that the hierarchy of sexual and moral values that governs the production of different sexualities privileges heterosexuality as engendering the "full range of human experience" (Vance, 1982: 282).

FLIRTING WITH THE "L" WORD

We have become used to the anchoring of images of different sexualities within popular culture through signifiers of taste, style, fashion, and glamour since the rise of so-called lesbian chic. The possible starting point of this trajectory is the 1993 cover shot in *Vanity Fair* of K.D. Lang, the out lesbian singer in a provocative pose with the supermodel Cindy Crawford, although as the discipline of lesbian studies has shown us any sense that lesbian visibility is linear and chronological should be approached with caution (Jagose, 2002; White, 1999). "Lesbian chic" has continued and gained momentum with the hyper-sexual images of the post-feminist heterosexual woman who teases the audience with her adventurous bravado. This might be signalled by her momentary same-sex kiss, which disappears in a puff of smoke or a breakdown in the pixels on the screen. This of course is one variant of the post-feminist woman who is not afraid to "try it out," not to appeal to male fantasy, but to position themselves as women with (sexual) agency, which they can enact in whatever way they damn well please. One interpretation that has become the mainstay of media commentary has been to foreground these representations as a positive improvement on earlier representations that have figured the lesbian as psychologically and socially inferior. The virtues of lesbian chic have been aligned with its potential to re-figure the lesbian as a "scandalous glamour object" (Briscoe 1994). The shadowy Other within this celebration becomes the lesbian who codes as butch and threatens heterosexuality through her border-crossing (Ciasullo, 2001). Rather than judge these representations for their veracity or authenticity I will consider the extent to which lesbian chic is offered as a (temporary) re/solution to the dilemmas and contradictions facing the heterosexual post-feminist woman.

FEMALE AGENCY

Female agency and its enactment has become a key concept that structures discussions of post-femininity (Probyn 1997; McRobbie, 2005). Women as sexual explorers, sexual adventurers, and sexual agents expand the landscape of representation offering women the injunction to choose how to be heterosexual and female. These fictional identities are re-making heterosexual femininity beyond patriarchal concerns, and privileging the capacity of women to be self-made, happy with singledom, and enacting their own agency as subjects. This exists alongside a range of cultural anxieties that contribute to what feminists such as Susan Bordo (1993) and Sarah Franklin (1997) have referred to as the "labor of femininity." This labor includes the continual emotional, psychological, and body work that provide the strategies and techniques through which women can re-invent themselves. Vance (1982: 4) discusses the relationships of "self-control and watchfulness" that women have been invited and incited to develop with themselves. She argues that these have been produced through a cultural ideology that positions women as the guardians of their own and other's (men's) sexuality. It would seem that rather than post-femininity offering a break from the past where female sexuality had to be protected and offered wardship, the post-feminist woman is entrapped within further dilemmas and contradictions that are deeply ambivalent and troubling. In order to understand the context that governs these dilemmas, discussions of female heterosexuality need to be shifted away from sex into an entirely different realm. The appeal of the "L" identity as a temporary resting place cannot be adequately understood through marking it as a place of sexual experimentation or desire (Lewis and Rolley, 1996). Although I will argue that sex is the surface signifier that frames representations of the hetero/lesbian, sex comes to stand in a metonymic relationship to the kinds of signifiers of relationship that the post-feminist woman is also required to disavow (Blackman, 2004).

UNTIL FURTHER NOTICE

Discussion of the reconfiguration of relationships and intimacy has become a central trope or metaphor for examining the new forms of subjectivity that are said to be emerging or have emerged within neo-liberalism (Bauman,

2003, Sennett, 2004, Beck and Beck-Gernsheim, 2000). Although I use the term neo-liberalism to refer to the forms of sociality now viewed as normative and desirable at the beginning of the twenty-first century, a diverse range of concepts are utilized by sociologists examining the psychological and political consequences of these forms (see Rose, 1996). Bauman (2003) uses the term "liquid love" to refer to the loosening or absence of kinship bonds he argues are characteristic of heterosexual intimate relationships. What characterizes relationships more than anything else he argues is their potential for ambivalence.[3] Bauman (2003) offers a very generalist reading of relationships that is rooted in the concept of the network. This notion captures what is seen to be the language of connectedness and disconnectedness used to frame relationship talk. This results in individuals judging others for their potential to fulfil their needs at a particular moment in time. Relationships are "communities of occasion" (Bauman, (2003: 32) offering temporary "comings together" (Bauman, 2003: 36), which are easily disposed by subjects as they attempt to negotiate a cultural injunction that invites them to be flexible and perpetually open to change. Bauman uses the idea of the "top pocket relationship" to describe relationships that are brought out when needed, and that one can leave relatively unscathed. Bauman sets the injunction of flexibility characteristic of neo-liberalism in opposition to cultural injunctions that would privilege and validate duty, commitment, and obligation, particularly in relationships. Thus relationships are disposable and part of the means through which subjects enact kinship bonds now governed by choice, flexibility, and self-making (Lury, 2002; Beck and Beck-Gernsheim, 2000). The flexible self is able to embrace change and movement, whereas the habitual self is aligned to rigidity, routine, and tradition, viewed as the enemy of flexibility (see Blackman, 2005).

Emily Martin (1994), in her fascinating study of the immune system, has argued that "flexibility" is a key explanatory structure that appears across a range of discourses and social practices. These include biomedical discussion of the immune system, systems theory, organizational and management practice, new age philosophy, self-help discourse, some forms of feminism, and some forms of psychological understanding. She suggests that we are all increasingly addressed as individuals who must be open to change and develop the skills to adapt to a shifting field of opportunities. The shadowy Other within this injunction is the notion of habit; where habits were once considered good friends or necessary adjuncts to routine, habits are now to be "let go" and "given up" in order to embrace potential. She argues that within this new cultural logic certain social groups may be seen as having rigid or unresponsive selves and bodies, making them relatively unfit for the kind of sociality we now seem to desire. Although Martin is particularly referring to the positioning of subjects in relation to their immune systems in the case of HIV, AIDS, and other auto-immune conditions, I want to develop some of these ideas to provide a framework for considering the importance of subjectivity. As a concept it provides a focus for investigating the ways in which differently sexed subjects enact and "hang together" a sense of coherence in the face of such a dialogic context. This context may go some way in explaining the conditions of emergence of new forms of sexed subjectivities where subjects enact or perform cultural norms that are marked by concepts of choice, autonomy, and agency. This might include the "post-gay," new cultural practices associated with queer youth culture, the hetero/lesbian and the polyamorous as specific enactments of the subject's desire to be open to expansion and change, as well as being able to live singularity in the face of multiplicity (Blackman, 2008b; Lee and Brown, 2002; Walkerdine, 2007).

The inclusion of a discussion of subjectivity within this article is an important reminder that what many sociologists are describing as a new cultural ontology of movement and flexibility, are becoming central to how many psychologists are differentiating normal psychological health from psychological economies viewed as symptomatic of psychopathology (Blackman, 2005). Those who lack the dialogic skills to be open to change and flexibility are viewed as more likely to experience mental health problems. Mental ill health is linked to rigidity, authoritarianism, stasis and fixity (Blackman, 2005). These accounts that traverse cultural theory and the psychological and biological sciences assume that the self is a process, not an entity, but that a healthy "self" is one who is capable of flexible re-organization and conscious discernment or deliberation. To be moved implies an awareness, and as Latour suggests in the context of what it means to have a body; to be put into motion requires a registering of this motion as, "if you are not engaged in this learning you become insensitive, dumb, you drop dead" (2004: 205). This posits a particular relationship between becoming and psychopathology that entirely ignores the relational connections and processes that articulate bodies in ways that are not easily seen or understood (Blackman, 2008). This also adds weight to Hemmings' (2005) argument that in the context of becoming and subjectivity, some "bodies are captured and held by affect's structured precision" whereas some are accorded *affective freedom* (p. 562).

HETERO/LESBIAN

It is the distinction between the flexible and habitual self that provides a cultural lens through which we might understand the social and psychological significance of representations of the *hetero/lesbian*. I will illustrate and develop this argument by considering some of the dilemmas and anxieties that govern these representations for the heterosexual woman encountering or considering lesbianism for the first time. As well as lesbians being anchored within images of glamour, style, fashion, and taste, another concept that structures the framework of visibility governing the emergence of "lesbian chic" is the concept of "waiting." Within this regime of representation, the usually heterosexual woman tries lesbianism whilest waiting for a man who is good enough. Whether Samantha in *Sex in the City* or Jessica in the film *Kissing Jessica Stein*, lesbianism is presented as a temporary fad for women to try who are tired of dating men who are not good enough. The endorsement given to the film *Kissing Jessica Stein* is that all the best men are either married or gay! The resolution for both narratives is that the relationships become sexless, and both return to their former heterosexual incarnations. As much as they can come out, they can always go back in. The kinds of narratives that construct their "coming out" episodes edit out the kinds of shame, feelings of humiliation, pain, guilt, and conflict that structure many "coming out" stories found in the lesbian and gay literature. Samantha announces over lunch, "Guess what, I am a lesbian," whereas Jessica's narrative is one of childlike immaturity where she is "found out" and redeemed through her marriage with her ex-fiancé who is ever-present throughout the narrative.

I want to suggest that there is a relationship between the anxieties and dilemmas of heterosexual post-femininity and the *hetero/lesbian*. This argument will be located within a study of lifestyle magazines.[4] The focus of the study was on how intimacy and relationship problems are both made intelligible and resolutions pro-offered across the categories of gender, race, and sexuality. I will relate some of the findings of this study to representations of the *hetero/lesbian* within popular culture more generally. I will argue that lesbianism becomes a temporary re/solution to the heterosexual woman's dilemma of waiting for a man who is good enough. This condenses a range of dilemmas and anxieties that govern heterosexual post-feminine identities. I argue elsewhere (Blackman, 2004, Blackman, in press) that the shift from romantic discourses governing femininity to those that advocate female self-determination are produced through cultural practices that encourage women to construct themselves as selves who can get by with relatively little support (Hochschild, 1994). This is alongside a disavowal of those signifiers of relationship associated with traditional or patriarchal femininity, including passivity, weakness, dependence, and so forth (see Hollway, 1984). This creates what Mick Billig (1997) has referred to as a "dialogic unconscious" embodying disavowed desires for warmth, comfort, security, and needing another. One key difference with patriarchal romantic resolutions is that the post-feminist woman is not figured as desperate or needy. In the following example, taken from the film *Kissing Jessica Stein*, the albeit temporary lesbian relationship provides some of the comforts that the heterosexual post-feminist woman is required to disavow, through her construction of herself as self-made. These include, for example, desires for emotional intimacy, security, and commitment (Blackman, 2004).

In one scene in the film, lesbianism is constructed as a glamorous fad, with the two lead characters in the film exchanging style tips and compliments. The construction of lesbianism as a particular taste or style is made explicit when Jessica exclaims, "I didn't realise that lesbians accessorised so much." This is a play on the cultural construction of the "lipstick lesbian" that disavows butchness, while enabling a discussion of whether they might choose sex toys as part of their sexual practices. On the surface sex becomes the signifier through which the girls enact their choice as sexual subjects. However, lesbianism also becomes a repository for all those desires and yearnings that the women have had to suppress in their string of hilariously unsuccessful heterosexual encounters. This includes the desire to be taken care of and looked after. This is epitomized in one scene where Jessica is looked after and given a special homemade soup by her female partner to help her recover from the flu. What is key to the heterosexual woman's negotiation of "lesbian chic" is the concept of choice; these women are enacting their capacity to be open to change and be flexible in the face of a range of co-existing opportunities. However, their negotiation of choice is governed by a range of dilemmas and anxieties that they have had to disavow in their construction of themselves as successful, independent subjects. Although on the surface these may appear contradictory they actually condense or conflate some of the principles that many feminists have argued govern post-femininity (Probyn, 1997).

FLEXIBLE SELFHOOD

What I am arguing is that these representations of the *hetero/lesbian* help to construct an image of the heterosexual woman or man as flexible and open to change, with the rigid lesbian who clings to her so-called pigeonholed labels as dreary and restricted. What this points toward is the omission in much of the sociological literature of exploring how sexed subject positions are enacted and embodied by different subjects who are addressed and negotiate these cultural injunctions in often glaringly different ways. The following example illustrates how the injunction of flexibility is translated within discussions of intimacy and relationships in gay and lesbian lifestyle magazines. In both lesbian and gay lifestyle magazines a key dilemma and contradiction governing the production of the autonomous, flexible self are the difficulties of being open and flexible in the face of homophobia and oppression. Although recognized that a relationship with oneself and others based on honesty, openness, and self-awareness is recognized as desirable, there is much discussion of the strategies of psychological preparedness and management that subjects are required to enact. These are primarily based on concealment, defensiveness, and deception. Often the narrative structure of "coming out'" narratives is based on a liberationist ethic charting a movement from this concealment to openness. The justification for these defensive strategies of self-management is the fear of violence, intimidation, and discrimination that forms the very real context of queer lives. Flexibility is therefore a nominal category, the meaning and practice of which is translated and produced in very different ways across the categories of gender, race, class, and sexuality.

What I am developing in my discussion so far are some different ways of beginning to understand the psychological and cultural significance of emergent forms of post-gay identities. It is clear that popular culture is structured by a kind of open and closed character (McRobbie, 2005). Different sexualities are constructed as an object of fear, loathing, and danger, alongside representations that construct different sexualities as an object of envy, desire, and yearning. In some senses this is nothing new and many writers have pointed to the ambivalence of lesbian and gay cultures of production and consumption (Butler, 1993, Plummer, 2001). What I want to argue however is that the salience of the production of lesbian sexuality as an object of taste, style, and glamour contain suppressed desires for emotional intimacy, commitment, and security. These exist in a metonymic relationship to sex that stands within these cultural texts as a surface signifier. I am suggesting that the kinds of cultural injunction that sociologists have identified as symptomatic of neo-liberalism are actually translated and embodied in very different ways across the categories of gender, race, class, and sexuality. As I have shown in the examples I have given, the injunctions are governed by very different dilemmas and cultural anxieties that position subjects in radically different ways in relation to the injunction of flexibility. What is clear is that the expansion of female and male heterosexuality to participate in cultures of consumption (including sexual and emotional consumption) aligned with homosexuality enrich the "psychology" of heterosexuality, while simultaneously aligning homosexuality with pathology and abnormality. This offers a new twist on the historical association of homosexuality with psychopathology. This time it is the distinction between the flexible and habitual self that affords the heterosexual a "break from routine" while fixing the homosexual within a relational complex marked by habit, rigidity, stasis, and psychosocial inferiority.

Beverley Skeggs (2004: 292) has described how such distinctions constitute who is considered a "subject of value" and is allowed access to and enabled to resource themselves and utilize sexualized (and gendered) practices as a way of enhancing their personhood. As she argues, "Others" are "denied their use because they are positioned *as* those classifications and are fixed by them" (Skeggs, 2004: 293). These complex positionings and the dilemmas and dialogic conscious[5] that they create form the background to the materiality of representational practices. This is a materiality that cannot be mapped onto the singular body, and yet is lived by individuals as they struggle to enact and "hang together" a coherent subjectivity in the face of multiplicity (see Blackman, 2008a). In current work I am exploring the value of the famous British anti-psychiatrist R.D. Laing's (1970) approach to affect and relationality as a way of exploring the production of subjectivities at the intersection of a complex set of relational connections, which he characterized through the concept of the *knot* (Blackman, 2008c). I am interested in how affects are transmitted and circulate across representational practices and what becomes placed in the background and silenced by (hetero)normative cultural logics. It is the dilemmas, contradictions, gaps, silences, and omissions produced by this that are of particular concern in analyzing the psychosocial dimensions of emergent "post-gay" subject positions. My aim in re-prioritizing analyses of the enactment and production of subjectivities is to explore how particular sexed subject positions enact, alter, emulate, disqualify, negate, or even invent new relationships to the cultural logic(s) of neo-liberalism and therefore relations to ourselves. In this project an examination of the cultural production of psychopathology is paramount, as it is those who become stuck by the proliferation and multiplication of positionings who suffer most from this logic of freedom, choice, and agency.

CONCLUSION

Celia Lury (2002: 589) has argued that at the very moment when the status of foundational concepts like nature and culture appear to be imploding or collapsing, "their distinctiveness continues to remain crucial." As identities become increasingly governed by an ethics of choice, new concepts are emerging for reinstating the distinctions between those bodies that are considered desirable and normative, and those that are relegated to a realm of psychopathology. On the one hand, emergent cultural representations of sexuality collapse sexual difference into style and taste affording an apparent de-naturalization of sexualities (see Franklin, Lury and Staceu, 2000). However, at the same time sexual difference becomes re-naturalized through a cultural ontology of movement and flexibility that naturalizes the enactment of choice in the making of identities. As Lury (2002) cogently argues this is a form of identity politics that connects different lifestyles with a life politics that provides new and novel ways of distinguishing difference. To add to this argument I would also wish to foreground the place of subjectivity in these kind-making processes. As we have seen from the example of the *hetero/lesbian*, the "hanging together" and enactment of subjectivities is crucial to understanding how different subjects live and survive these new cultural ontologies. What needs urgent attention are the ways in which lesbian, gay, bisexual, and transgender (LGBT) subjects are negotiating this new sexual landscape, and what kinds of narratives and practices are covered over, silenced, elided, and eclipsed by the collapse of sexual difference into style, taste, and a temporary resting place. If we remain at the level of representation the complexity of our being and becoming will be covered over by the apparent glamour, gloss, and choice of this newly sexed landscape.

NOTES

1. The approach I am trying to develop toward subjectivity is one that rejects "psychological individualism" and yet does point to the ways in which subjects attempt to live singularity in the face of multiplicity. This is what I have termed the problem of the "one and the many"; how subjects can be multiple and singular and the complex processes of self-production that are enacted in order to "hang together" (Blackman et al., 2008; Blackman, 2008a). The accomplishment or achievement of subjectivity is thus always a thoroughly relational and affective process.

2. Claire Hemmings (2005) has cogently foregrounded the current interest in affect as one that promises to emancipate the subject from social constraint, and thus to sideline theories and (paranoid) theorists who might wish to explore affect as an enduring mechanism of social reproduction. Thus "good affect" is that which is taken to "undo" whereas "bad affect" is that which sticks, fixes, and prevents movement and change.

3. "[R]elationships are perhaps the most common, acute, deeply felt and troublesome incarnations of ambivalence" (Bauman, 2003: viii).

4. This study was funded by the Arts and Humanities Research Board, "Inventing the Psychological: Lifestyle Magazines and the Fiction of Autonomous Selfhood" (AN6596/APN10894). My thanks to the research assistant, Dr. Laura Miller.

5. As Billig argues, "the meaning of any utterance, or piece of logos, must be understood in terms of its dialogical context, and this means in terms of the anti-logos, which it seeks to counter" (Billig, 1997: 225).

REFERENCES

Bauman, Z. *Liquid Love: On the Frailty of Human Bonds*. Cambridge: Polity, 2003.

Beck, U. and E. Beck-Gernsheim. *Individualization*. London: Sage, 2000.

Bhabha, H. *The Location of Culture*. London: Routledge, 1994.

Billig, M. "Cultural Studies, Discourse and Psychology: From Codes to Utterances." In M. Ferguson and P. Golding, eds. *Cultural Studies in Question*. London: Sage, 1997: 205–227.

Blackman, L. "Self-Help, Media Cultures and the Problem of Female Psychopathology." *European Journal of Cultural Studies*, 7(2), 2004: 241–58.

———. "The Dialogic Self: Flexibility and the Cultural Production of Psychopathology." *Theory and Psychology*, 15(2), 2005: 182–206.

———. "Inventing the Psychological: Lifestyle Magazines and the Fiction of Autonomous Selfhood." In J. Curran and D. Morley, eds. *Media and Cultural Theory*. London and New York: Routledge, 2006: 209–220.

———. "Affect, Relationality and the Problem of Personality." *Theory, Culture and Society*, 25(1), 2008a: 27–51.

———. *The Body: The Key Concepts*. Oxford and New York: Berg, 2008b.

———. "Is Happiness Contagious?" *New Formations: Special Issue on Happiness edited by S. Ahmed*. Issue 63, 2008c: 15–32.

———. "It's Down to You: Psychology, Magazine Culture and the Governing of Female Bodies." In P. Saukko, ed. *Governing the Female Body*. Albany: State University of New York Press (in press).

———, J. Cromby, D. Hook, D. Papadopoulous, and V. Walkerdine. "Editorial: Creating Subjectivities." *Subjectivity*, 22, 2008: 1–27.

——— and V. Walkerdine. *Mass Hysteria: Critical Psychology and Media Studies*. Basingstoke and New York: Palgrave, 2001.

Bordo, S. *Unbearable Weight: Feminism, Western Culture and the Body*. Berkeley: University of California Press, 1993.

Braidotti, R. *Metamorphoses: Towards a Materialist Theory of Becoming*. Oxford: Polity Press, 2002.

Braidotti, R. *Transpositions*. Cambridge: Polity, 2006.

Briscoe, J. "Lesbians Hard Sell." *Elle, May*, 1994: 57–60.

Butler, J. *Bodies that Matter: On the Discursive Limits of "Sex."* London and New York: Routledge, 1993.

Ciasullo, A. M. "Making Her (In)Visible: Cultural Representations of Lesbianism and the Lesbian Body in the 1990's." *Feminist Studies*, *27*(3), 2001: 577–608.

Clough, P. "Introduction." In P. Clough with J. Halley, eds. *The Affective Turn: Theorizing the Social*. Durham and London: Duke University Press, 2007: 1–33.

Driver, S. *Queer Youth Cultures*. Albany: SUNY University Press, 2008.

Franklin, S. *Embodied Progress. A Cultural Account of Assisted Conception*. London: Routledge, 1997.

————, C. Lury, and J. Stacey. *Global Nature, Global Culture*. London: Sage, 2000.

Gil, R. *Gender and the Media*. Cambridge: Polity, 2006.

Halberstam, J. *Female Masculinity*. London and Durham, NC: Duke University Press, 1998.

Hemmings, C. "Invoking Affect: Cultural Theory and the Ontological Turn." *Cultural Studies*, *19*(5), 2005: 548–567.

Hochschild, A. "The Commercial Spirit of Intimate Life and the Abduction of Feminism: Signs from Women's Advice Books." *Theory, Culture and Society*, *11*, 1994: 1–24.

Hollway, W. "Gender Difference and the Production of Subjectivity." In J. Henriques, W. Hollway, C. Urwin, C. Venn and V. Walkerdine, eds. *Changing the Subject. Psychology, Social Regulation and Subjectivity*. London: Methuen, 1984: 227–263.

Jagose, A. *Inconsequence: Lesbian Representation and the Logic of Sexual Sequence*. Ithaca and London: Cornell University Press, 2002.

Laing, R. D. *Knots*. New York: Pantheon Books, 1970.

Latour, B. "How to Talk About the Body? The Normative Dimensions of Science Studies." *Body and Society*, *10*(2–3), 2004: 205–230.

Lee, N. and S. Brown. "The Disposal of Fear: Childhood, Trauma and Complexity." In J. Law and A. Mol, eds. *Complexities: Social Studies of Knowledge Practices*. Durham and New York: Duke University Press, 2002: 258–280.

Lewis, R. and K. Rolley. "Ad(dressing) the Dyke: Lesbian Looks and Lesbians Looking." In P. Horne and R. Lewis, eds. *Outlooks: Lesbian and Gay Sexualities and Visual Cultures*. London and New York: Routledge, 1996: 178–190.

Lury, C. "From Diversity to Heterogeneity: A Feminist Analysis of the Making of Kinds." *Economy and Society*, *4*, 2002: 588–605.

Martin, E. *Flexible Bodies: The Role of Immunity in American Culture from the Days of Polio to the Age of Aids*. Boston, MA: Beacon Press, 1994.

McRobbie, A. *The Uses of Cultural Studies*. London: Sage, 2005.

Mort, F. *Dangerous Sexualities: Medico-moral Politics in England since 1830*. London: Routledge and Kegan Paul, 1987.

Nixon, S. "Resignifying Masculinity: From 'New Man' to 'New Lad.'" In D. Morley and K. Robins, eds. *British Cultural Studies*. New York and Oxford: Oxford University Press, 2001: 373–386.

Plummer, K. "Gay Cultures/Straight Borders." In D. Morley and K. Robins, eds. *British Cultural Studies*. New York and Oxford: Oxford University Press, 2001: 387–398.

Probyn, E. "New Traditionalism and Postfeminism: TV Does the Home." In C. Brunsdon, J. D'Acci, and L. Segal, eds. *Feminist Television Criticism: A Reader*. Oxford: Clarendon, 1997.

Prosser, J. *Second Skins: The Body Narratives of Transsexuality*. New York: Columbia University Press, 1998.

Rose, N. *Inventing Ourselves. Psychology, Power and Personhood*. Cambridge, New York, and Melbourne: Cambridge University Press, 1996.

Sennett, R. *Respect: The Formation of Character in an Age of Inequality*. London: Penguin, 2004.

Skeggs, B. "Uneasy Alignments. Resourcing Respectable Subjectivity." *GLQ: A Journal of Lesbian and Gay Studies, 10*(2), 2004: 291–298.

Vance, C. *Pleasure and Danger: Exploring a Politics of Sexuality*. Boston, MA: Routledge and Kegan Paul, 1982.

Walkerdine, V., H. Lucey, and J. Melody. *Growing Up Girl. Psychosocial Explorations of Gender and Class*. Basingstoke and New York: Palgrave, 2001.

———. *Children, Gender, Video Games*. Basingstoke and New York: Palgrave, 2007.

White, P. *UnInvited: Classical Hollywood Cinema and Lesbian Representability*. Bloomington and Indianapolis: Indiana University Press, 1999.

Williams, R. *Marxism and Literature*. Oxford: Oxford University Press, 1977.

The Lady Vanishes: On Never Knowing, Quite, Who Is a Lesbian

KATH WESTON

Researchers, like political contestants, have to engage matters of epistemology to frame their claims and their debates. In that sense the emerging consensus between lesbian, gay, bisexual, transgender, and queer (LGBTQ) advocates and their political adversaries that it is impossible to recognize lesbians by sight, much less indexically gendered features, is instructive. This article reviews a range of methodological research strategies designed to grapple with the complexities of determining who counts as "lesbian" in different contexts. Those classificatory strategies include working definitions, self-definition, identification of "bias," interpretive embrace of slippery categories, and turning the process of classification into an object of study. After exploring the strengths and shortcomings of each approach, the article argues for a calculus of belonging based on the concept of limit rather than a politics of demarcation.

Every so often, opposites do more than attract: they converge. During the Cold War, for example, antagonists who adhered to very different political ideologies pursued similarly modernist, often utopian dreams of progress (Buck-Morss, 2000). During the "Troubles" in Ireland, the tactics of the Irish Republic Army and their adversaries developed an eerie resemblance, symbolized by the balaclavas that both groups donned for their operations (Aretxaga, 1997). Another kind of convergence occurred in the 1970s, when gay liberationists went head-to-head with Christian fundamentalists in the United States over the issue of whether homosexuality should be sanctioned. A vexed consensus gradually emerged in response to one of the oldest questions in the book of contemporary sexual politics: How do you tell who is lesbian or gay?

At the time, movement activists had gone to great lengths to educate the public about what they termed the "myth" that lesbians are inevitably butch and gay men invariably effeminate. Not every lesbian looks like she drives a big rig, they patiently explained. Not every gay man spends his evenings practicing the moves required to lip-synch his way to fame in a drag show. Queers hail from every walk of life and may or may not gender-bend. Moral: Heterosexuals who are convinced that they have never met a lesbian should probably think twice. While activists hammered away on these points, an illustrated religious pamphlet called "The Gay Blade" (n.d.: 6) was making its way from hand to hand throughout the country. Do not be fooled, its anonymous authors warned: "They occupy all kinds of jobs. Their identity for the most part is carefully hidden." A lesbian can be as feminine as the next woman. Gay teenagers can look like the boy next door. Indeed, they might *be* the kids next door. Unfortunately for the unsuspecting fundamentalist devotee, you cannot always know them when you see them.

The pedagogical prescriptions that these contending views of homosexuality promoted called for enlightened acceptance, on the one hand, and enlightened condemnation, on the other, but the methodological implication was the same. It's hard—nay, impossible—to tell who is queer, at least from any superficial inspection.

Of course, that does not stop people from trying. Even social scientists, who tend to position themselves above the ragtag battles of popular culture, all the better to study them, grapple with a pressing need to identify the subject/object of analysis. For investigations of lesbians in the workplace (or bisexual relationships, or sexual surveillance, or transgender politics, or what have you), definitions and parameters would seem essential. How else to know whom to study? How else to formulate generalizations? How else to determine what's worth scrutiny, who's eligible for inclusion, and who's just pulling your leg?

The pitfalls of attempting to arrive at a definitive answer in this matter are well known, although often conveniently ignored when there's a chance to make a profit. Take the frequently reiterated generalization that "gay people" are wealthier than the average denizen of the United States. Salespeople have used this contention, clothed as fact, on the one hand, and the fruit of careful study, on the other, to sell advertisements in the glossy lifestyle magazines aimed at people who identify with at least one of the letters in the acronym "LGBTQ" (lesbian, gay, bisexual, transgender, and queer). In her essay, "Beyond Biased Samples: Challenging the Myths on the Economic Status of Lesbians and Gay Men," M.V. Lee Badgett (1997) traced at least some such claims to the results of survey data collected by marketing research companies from readers of those very magazines and newspapers.[1] A methodology of this sort is self-serving at worst and dubious at best, because readers of a middle-class consumer-oriented publication who take the time to fill out a questionnaire hardly comprise a representative sample, without even going into the matter of what exactly they are supposed to be representing. Nonetheless, such surveys can lend an aura of scientific backing to already existing resentments.

If you think conducting research "on lesbians" is hard, imagine being a young woman of limited means with a crush on her girlfriend who is trying to dream herself into a sense of belonging. "Are there other people like me?" she wonders. (What would I ever have to say to those smug ladies with perfect teeth in the magazine?) "Am I a lesbian?" (Considering that I cannot afford the advertised lesbian adventure cruise, and would go out of my mind being marooned on a ship in a sea of white faces besides?)

One could argue that "better" survey data would have put paid to poorly backed generalizations about the nexus of class/sexuality, and quickly. Yet surveys are nothing without demographics. It is notoriously difficult even to hazard a guess at the demographics of a group that (like many groups) is an amalgam with no fixed boundaries, a group that (unlike many groups) embraces shifting, contextual forms of closeting. What you tell Mom may be different from what you tell Uncle Frank, what you told yourself when you were thirteen, how you portray yourself to prospective employers, what affiliations you'll claim when you're sixty, and what you intimate to your date. To make things more complicated, when categories such as "lesbian," "gay," or "tomboy" circulate globally, they acquire different nuances and meanings as they take up new lives in various locations.[2] Florence Babb (2003), for instance, explores how the Nicaraguan Revolution created a context in which homosexual politics—including transnational "lesbian and gay" politics—unfolded differently than in avowedly capitalist societies such as the United States. Add to this the complexities of the nationalist, religious, racial, and class politics of naming and claiming belonging; stir in a measure of doubt regarding the criteria (behavior? association? identity?) used to classify someone as "a lesbian"; throw in a dose of historical change for good measure; and you have yourself a recipe for uncertainty.

Since the emergence of LGBTQ studies, there have been many approaches to resolving the researcher's dilemma of a subject/object who insists on vanishing into shifting, sometimes conflicting definitions. In what follows, I briefly review some of the more prominent methodological strategies and discuss their epistemological limitations. I show why, although serviceable, these approaches remain limited, although not necessarily in a bad way. Rather than searching for some unassailable definition of who should count as a lesbian or lamenting the limitations associated with any provisional answer, I suggest refiguring the notion of the limit itself. A limit need not always imply constriction, inadequacy, bias, partiality, or regrettable constraint. In calculus the limit carries an infinitely expansive sense of something just beyond, approachable although never reached. Directed movement, not arrival or attainment, lends calculus its considerable power. In that sense of a limit lies an opportunity to embrace the "never quite" in "never quite knowing," in such a way that insights can spring from the very movements that shuttle bodies between categories with shifting meanings: now lesbian, now silent, now queer, now "tomboy" (in English), now "tomboi" (in Tagalog), now "happening to fall in love with a woman," now "whatever you want to call me."

DEFINITIONS, WORKING OR OTHERWISE

Classification is an enterprise steeped in meaning, so it comes as no surprise that the "sexualities" taken as objects of study can prove slippery, when not sliding from view altogether. The research conducted on sexualities also has a part in articulating them, reifying them, and thus making them what they are.[3] Like the photons memorialized in descriptions of the observer effect, which bombard electrons during the course of observation and shift their path, effectively altering the phenomenon under investigation, your questions ensure that, following the interview, "Lesbian X" will not be exactly the same person whose words you recorded. Nor will she be located, or locatable, in the very same social space in which you thought you saw her. Social relations are fluid for reasons that include the scholarly encounter. So if research is to proceed in any *meaningful* way, what is to be done?

The strategies that researchers historically have put into play to capture a glimpse of the ever-vanishing lesbian include adopting a working definition, relying on self-identification, treating the methodological challenges as a matter of "bias" or compromised objectivity, refining their questions to allow for slippery categories, and transforming the fool's errand of attempting to definitively know someone's sexual identity into the object of analysis. Each of these sometimes incompatible strategies has something to recommend it. Each also features drawbacks, complications, and caveats that can call into question the value of a study.

Suppose, for example, Professor C.V. Itis decides to adopt a working definition of who will count as a lesbian for the purposes of her latest research into the effects of government budget cuts on the animal–human relationships pursued by lesbian forest rangers in an era of global warming. (Just kidding, of course, but suppose.) Her definition is likely to be based on criteria determined by the researcher and applied from the researcher's side. She might qualify women for her study based on number of previous sexual encounters with another woman, involvement in a relationship with another woman, self-identification as a lesbian, self-identification as a lesbian at some point in the past, having come out as a lesbian to one's closest friend, or any number of other possible criteria, plus employment as a ranger. But will her working definition work? That depends on what you consider a successful research strategy and what you expect to come out of the research.

Working definitions have the apparent advantage of precision and consistency in their application. Yet those virtues often prove illusory, because working definitions tend to be at once rather arbitrary, on the one hand, and culture-bound, on the other. A working definition based on number of sexual encounters must specify how many. But what is the rationale for choosing, say, three over one or eight? What counts as a "sexual encounter," anyway? (A question whose answer is no more obvious than who counts as a lesbian.) How many encounters add up to a "sexual history"? Should kissing another woman count? Should the researcher make an exception for a really *good* kisser? That is to say, do qualitative assessments based on the researcher's judgment have a place in constructing her working definitions?

Likewise, a criterion that requires participants to be in a same-sex relationship will miss both celibate women who consider themselves lesbians and women whose erotic entanglements do not take the form of relationships. It may also miss women who call themselves lesbians but also believe that lesbian identity is about much more than eroticism. A researcher might be able to live with those omissions, but she needs to be cognizant of them and reflective about how they shape her results. Even then, awareness of the limitations of working definitions does not offer guidance to the researcher struggling with the rationales for weighing one criterion more heavily than another as she constructs her selection criteria. A study from the 1990s by Paula Rust, for example, found that women who called themselves lesbian and women who called themselves bisexual had "a wide range of sexual experience common to both groups" (1992: 366). A working definition that gave more weight to behavior than identity might not catch the difference, nor could it grasp whether that difference made a difference to the women concerned.

What's more, the criteria that suggest themselves to a researcher as good candidates for incorporation into a working definition do not fall into the researcher's hands from some review board in the sky. They generally come from a combination of tacit knowledge, always culturally conceived, and intellectual legacies and disciplinary habits that influence where a researcher looks when she casts about for definitions. A researcher must start somewhere, but working with vaguely articulated cultural equations of what "lesbians" are all about (e.g., lesbian = sex, so focus on intimacy or eroticism) can shift any study toward what researchers already think they know.[4] If you ask about sex, then sex is probably what you will hear about from anyone who agrees to talk to you. But that does not mean that sex lies at the heart of her claim to the category "lesbian" in the way that she understands it.

These shortcomings of working definitions illustrate some of the reasons why many researchers have resorted to using self-identification as a stand-alone qualification. If a person calls herself a lesbian, then she is one, for the purposes of the study, regardless of what she has or has not done by any behavioral measure. In one sense, of course, self-identification is just another working definition, but here the criterion has been elevated to a privileged arbiter of inclusion.

Self-identification has more than one quality to recommend it to researchers on a quest for the grail of the lesbian subject. Unlike behavioral measures, self-identification links any insights that emerge from a study to the meaningful constitution of sexual identities, that is to say, to the way that the subjects themselves mobilize, interpret, and lay claim to classification as a "lesbian." In theory, at least, self-identification frees the research *subject's* understanding from its previous *subjection* to the understanding, prejudices, and whims of the researcher. This is a capacious strategy that allows "lesbian" to signify different things to different people. This is also a strategy that traces its lineage to debates about power politics, feminist methodology, and feminist ethnography more particularly. By giving more "voice" to the people being studied, researchers hoped to ameliorate some of the inequality built into the researcher/researched relationship.[5]

Now what could possibly be wanting in a strategy that accords the subject respect by granting her the power to determine her own eligibility for study? There is a line of critique that convincingly argues that the egalitarian thrust of feminist methodology has not lived up to its billing, not for lack of trying, but simply because the researcher/researched relationship incarnates a power differential that no amount of respect can dispel. The investigator who allows "her subjects" to self-identify as lesbians (or what have you) is still the one doing the allowing. The scholar who "gives voice" to the people in her studies is still the one who selects participants (however self-identified), edits her transcripts, pulls out quotes from interviews to illustrate her theses, and otherwise creates the narrative voice that appears in print. Nor did feminist methodology turn out to be as distinctively feminist as some of its advocates claimed. Methodologies developed in association with critical race theory, for example, enlisted many of the same tactics for redressing inequality.[6]

There are ontological critiques of self-identification that can also be mustered that go to the heart of the "problem" of the vanishing lesbian. Suppose, as many philosophers have contended, that the self is not a unified entity with continuity over time. Suppose, as many anthropologists have contended, the notion of a bounded self is exceedingly culture-bound, a site-specific construct that would seem strange, even nonsensical, to people living under other circumstances. What then? If there is no unified, continuous self, who is it who does the "self"-identifying? If the bounded self is but a powerful figment of history, political economy, and culture, how best to approach "sexualities" in other times and places? And to the extent that radically individualist notions of bounded selves are just that—notions—how can investigators take into account the collective contribution to anyone's "self"-definition?

The implications of these ontological critiques for research are not trivial. As Arlene Stein (1997) noted in "Sleeping with the Enemy? Ex-Lesbians and the Reconstruction of Identity," women's identifications can shift over the course of their lives.[7] One could argue that such temporal shifts pose a conundrum for research—not to mention a woman's peers—precisely because the self credited with doing the identifying has been accorded a kind of essence and stability.

Because self-definition, by definition, also permits anyone to lay claim to lesbian identity, the results can be at odds with so-called common-sense understandings of the term. In one of the early seasons of the television drama *The L Word*, a male character who insisted he identified as a lesbian struck up a relationship with a female character who had a history of erotic involvement with other women. Much of the tension and humor in ensuing episodes revolved around her friends' struggles to come to terms with the relationship. Should they accept the "male lesbian's" account of his own sexuality? Can there be such a thing as a man who is a lesbian? If he identifies as a lesbian is he "really" a man? Was their friend in a lesbian relationship, or would that depend on how she viewed her partner's sexual identity? Should they give weight to motive and instrumentalism in making their classification? That is to say, what would the truth of his claim be if he only gave this account of himself to get her into bed? Their discomfiture underlines the point that sexualities are socially negotiated, never just our own, a key aspect that self-identification misses when used as a privileged criterion.

Perhaps the most popular approach to studying the vanishing subject/object known as the lesbian is to acknowledge such methodological problems, then treat them as a regrettable bias and allow a margin for error. Yes, it's frightfully Cartesian to privilege self-identification on the grounds that we are all supposed to know ourselves the best, but research has to begin somewhere. Let's acknowledge the shortcomings of whatever research strategy we adopt, try to minimize them, and get on with it. Yet the very notion of bias incorporated into what could be called the "minimize bias" approach holds fast to a notion of objectivity, the elusive ideal from which every mortal study must depart. This, Renato Rosaldo (1993) contends, may represent the researcher's most telling gaffe. What objectivist researchers are taught to dismiss as bias becomes instead, for Rosaldo, the very font of creativity and comprehension. If you want to gauge the *significance* of the way that Professor C.V. Itis' lesbian rangers relate to animal life in the rapidly heating forest, you would be better off thinking about how to account for what you apprehended during the time you spent with them. The ensuing analysis might record your own stumbles en route to understanding, as well as your best sense of what in the world these women meant when they used words such as "down time," "campfire," "*hermana*," "staff cut," and "marshmallow s'more." Far from constituting a source of regret, the element of interpretation built into research, which renders categories such as "lesbian" indeterminate, represents its most intriguing characteristic.

Typically there's more attention given to symbols and meanings than material exchanges in interpretive accounts.[8] They work hard to contextualize analysis by posing clarifying questions. ("You say you consider "lesbian" and "queer" to be different, but different with respect to what?") They pay heed to the researcher effect, often writing reflexively about the investigator's experience while conducting the study. They tend to be cognizant that research subjects, like researchers, can be implicated in the way that the events they describe unfold. But if, say, political economy is at the heart of what you hoped to comprehend, you will not find as many methodological tools at your disposal with this strategy. Through it all, the lady is still vanishing. It's just that, with the interpretive approach, there's something to be learned from the trick.

Enter an entire genre of studies that have turned the impossibility of ever knowing who's a lesbian into the object of analysis. Or rather, a genre that transforms the negotiations that produce sexual classification into the very phenomenon under examination. Lisa Walker's (1993) essay, "How to Recognize a Lesbian: The Cultural Politics of Looking Like What You Are," would be a case in point. Eithne Luibheid's (1998, 2002) research on assessments of sexual identity by immigration agents at the United States/Mexico border would be another. Because the drawing of any line creates an inside and an outside, an exclusion for every inclusion, the process is necessarily politicized. As a research strategy this one is clever, insightful, and seemingly infinite in its applications, but it hardly begins to tap the range of possibilities for study.

Most researchers have a less recursive project in mind when they set out to study something about "lesbians." Suppose they simply (or not so simply) want to study the division of labor in lesbian households at a time when jobs demand more and more of people's time. Or lesbian leadership in environmental justice movements. Or lesbian involvement with "sanctified" churches. Or the commodification of sexual identity in advertisements pitched to a lesbian audience. Or the publication of a "lesbian" newsletter in Brazil. Or the history of participation by lesbians of color in so-called white women's movements in the United States. Or the struggle by Two Spirits on the Diné reservation to overturn the Navajo Nation Council's ban on "gay marriage." Or the effects of tighter immigration controls on relationships with a same-sex partner's family. In practical terms, what does it mean to get on with the research? Is there a way to proceed without wrestling the category "lesbian" into a box of meanings that keeps the light away from the very features you had hoped to glimpse?

SUNYATA BETWEEN THE SHEETS

What if there was an epistemological strategy that did not require a researcher to place parameters around a category such as lesbian, the better to know it, yet also did not limit studies to a focus on the process of knowing itself? Is it possible to inhabit an epistemological stance that tarries with the category "lesbian" in the course of developing a range of vibrant methodologies for pursuing "lesbian studies," yet does not seek to capture the category for research?

Clearly, reliance on the trope of visibility will not do. Knowing one when you see one offers no better guide than knowing one when you hear one, touch one, or, for that matter, define one. Likewise for the trope of identity, individually reported and construed. Suppose, instead, we zero in for a moment on the "quite" in "never knowing, quite, who is a lesbian." In this formulation, the never-quite-known (or knowable) lesbian is not a stable, bounded person or a thing but a category of convenience for describing a process of constant re-worlding that now here, now there, works a little something called "*tomboi*," "femme," "Two Spirit," "best friend," "gay marriage," "*tortillera*," "workplace discrimination," "*bading*," "roommate," or "sexuality" into the flow. Knowledge becomes a limit that a researcher can use these terms to approach but not attain.

Like all categories, "lesbian" holds *sunyata*, zero, emptiness, at its heart, rather than any definite play of meanings. *Sunyata* inhabits the flash of uncertainty when meanings come undone, for the fundamentalist, the activist, the investigator, or the prospective subject/object of research. Is she or isn't she? Does the category apply to me or not? In *Gender in Real Time: Power and Transience in a Visual Age*, I discuss at greater length the part that *sunya*, the zero, plays in signification:

> Zero operates as a meta-sign: both a sign *about* signs, and a sign for the *absence* of other signs. If zero is there, seven is not there; in the place where zero stands, two and forty-seven are not. . . . [Z]ero signifies not only an absence, but also the potential for later occupation. Movement is thus implicit in the sign. Zero also keeps other numerals in their place, so to speak. By occupying a position in a certain order, a zero endows that position with value, while changing the value of adjoining numbers accordingly. (2002: 39)

Think of the difference between ten (10) euros and one million (1,000,000) euros, and the process of valuation linked to *sunya*, the zero, becomes obvious.

In everyday life, people often apprehend *sunyata* through a fleeting sense of something they had previously thought was fixed coming undone. That sense brings with it feelings of movement, revaluation, and uncertainty with respect to gender, race, kinship, sexuality, or whatever category the researcher is trying so diligently to grasp. But this need not be a reason to throw up her hands in epistemological despair. Sexualities cannot coalesce, however transiently, however indifferently, as identities, behaviors, indeed, *as such*, without this perpetual emptying out.

This is not a matter of a "bias" built into the analysis, nor is it your unmarried aunt's cultural relativism. *Sunyata* does not take on the interpretive task of weighing and investigating meanings, although being empty of intrinsic meaning, *sunyata* also does not exclude it. Working with *sunyata* entails cultivating an understanding of the place momentarily held open for meanings to take shape, transform, come and go. Doing so requires a researcher to distinguish the desire to know from the desire to pin down, to abandon nostalgia for the perfect Euclidean contours of the golden circle, for the reign of definitions and heavenly forms. Instead of modeling research on a quest narrative, on the naturalist's perusal of butterflies staked to a board, on the militarist's battleground map of strategy, researchers attend to the vanishing. With that in mind, they make a start.

In a twist on the old adage, regardless of how solidly a research subject presents on the streets, it's *sunyata* between the sheets.[9] Whatever "lesbian" may connote in any provisional sense, by the time you qualify her as a research participant she'll be looking rather, well, lesbian. To you, anyway. She may even parse her subjective sense of a lesbian self into words to reassure the conscientious investigator. And that's when she will be gone.

NOTES

1. See also the essay "The Gay Marketing Moment" by Amy Gluckman and Betsy Reed (1997) in the same volume.

2. See, for example, Rofel (1999) on China and Blackwood (1998) and Boellstorff (2005) on Indonesia, Manalansan (1997) on the Filipino/a diaspora, and Puar (2001) on Trinidad. Where these authors differ is in their analysis of the dialectic between local categories and transnationally circulating terms such as "lesbian," as well as transnational LGBTQ politics more generally.

3. On the reification of sexuality in the course of its study, see Weston (1998).

4. Judith Bennett's (2000) concept of "lesbian-like," advanced to address the challenges of studying same-sex intimacy in historical eras for which "lesbian" represents an anachronism, recognizes more clearly than most the instability of categories. Yet Bennett's analysis has the paradoxical effect of recuperating an unmarked coherence and continuity into her categories by linking earlier intimacies back to "lesbian" through the notion of similarity.

5. For a sense of classic opening debates on feminist methodology, see Stacey (1988), Stanley and Wise (1983), and Strathern (1987). For a sense of more recent extensions and elaborations of those debates, see Maynard and Purvis (1994) and Hesse-Biber and Yaiser (2004).

6. Discussions of the effects of situated knowledge incorporated into research by "native ethnographers" in contexts marked by conflict and inequality are also relevant here (see, e.g., Abu-Lughod, 1992; Back and Keith, 1999; Frankenberg, 1993; Jackson, 2005; Jones, 1970; Lewin and Leap, 1996; Narayan, 1993; Ware and Back, 2001; and Weston, 1998).

7. Chapter six of Stein's *Sex and Sensibility* (1997).

8. The literature on the interpretive turn in anthropology is vast, but in addition to Rosaldo, one might start with Geertz (2000) and Panourgiá and Marcus (2008). For examples of ethnographies that attempt to integrate some of the idealist concerns of interpretive analysis into studies that focus on political economy, see Taussig (1983), Venkatesh (2006), Wacquant (2004), and Weston (2002).

9. The adage here being, of course, "butch in the streets, femme in the sheets."

REFERENCES

Abu-Lughod, Lila. *Writing Women's Worlds: Bedouin Stories*. Berkeley: University of California Press, 1992.

Aretxaga, Begoña. *Shattering Silence: Women, Nationalism, and Political Subjectivity in Northern Ireland*. Princeton, NJ: Princeton University Press, 1997.

Babb, Florence E. "Out in Nicaragua: Local and Transnational Desires after the Revolution." *Cultural Anthropology, 18*(3), 2003: 304–328.

Back, Les and Michael Keith. "'Rights and Wrongs': Youth, Community, and Narratives of Racial Violence." In Phil Cohen, ed. *New Ethnicities, Old Racisms*. London: Zed Books, 1999.

Badgett, M. V. Lee. "Beyond Biased Samples: Challenging the Myths on the Economic Status of Lesbians and Gay Men." In Amy Gluckman and Betsy Reed, eds. *Homo Economics: Capitalism, Community, and Lesbian and Gay Life*. New York: Routledge, 1997: 65–72.

Bennett, Judith M. "'Lesbian-Like' and the Social History of Lesbianisms." *Journal of the History of Sexuality, 9*(1–2), 2000: 1–24.

Blackwood, Evelyn. "*Tombois* in West Sumatra: Constructing Masculinity and Erotic Desire." *Cultural Anthropology, 13*(4), 1998: 491–521.

Boellstorff, Tom. *The Gay Archipelago: Sexuality and Nation in Indonesia*. Princeton, NJ: Princeton University Press, 2005.

Buck-Morss, Susan. *Dreamworld and Catastrophe: The Passing of Mass Utopia in East and West*. Cambridge, MA: MIT Press, 2000.

Frankenberg, Ruth. *White Women, Race Matters: The Social Construction of Whiteness*. New York: Routledge, 1993.

"The Gay Blade." Anonymous pamphlet reproduced online at http://www.brumm.com/gaylib/gayblade/index.html, n.d. (accessed February 23, 2008).

Geertz, Clifford. *Local Knowledge: Further Essays in Interpretive Anthropology*. New York: Basic Books, 2000.

Gluckman, Amy and Betsy Reed. 1997. "The Gay Marketing Moment." In Amy Gluckman and Betsy Reed, eds. *Homo Economics: Capitalism, Community, and Lesbian and Gay Life*. New York: Routledge, 1997: 3–9.

Hesse-Biber, Sharlene Nagy and Michelle L. Yaiser, eds. *Feminist Perspectives on Social Research*. New York: Oxford University Press, 2004.

Jackson, John L. *Real Black: Adventures in Racial Sincerity*. Chicago: University of Chicago Press, 2005.

Jones, Delmos J. "Towards a Native Anthropology." *Human Organization, 29*(4), 1970: 251–259.

Lewin, Ellen and William L. Leap, eds. *Out in the Field: Reflections of Lesbian and Gay Anthropologists*. Urbana: University of Illinois Press, 1996.

Luibheid, Eithne. *Entry Denied: Controlling Sexuality at the Border.* Minneapolis: University of Minnesota Press, 2002.

––––––––––. "'Looking like a Lesbian': The Organization of Sexual Monitoring at the United States-Mexican Border." *Journal of the History of Sexuality, 8*(3), 1998: 477–506.

Manalansan, Martin F. "In the Shadows of Stonewall: Examining Gay Transnational Politics and the Diasporic Dilemma." In Lisa Lowe and David Lloyd, eds. *The Politics of Culture in the Shadow of Capital.* Durham, NC: Duke University Press, 1997: 485–505.

Maynard, Mary and June Purvis, eds. *Researching Women's Lives from a Feminist Perspective.* London: Taylor & Francis, 1994.

Narayan, Kirin. "How Native Is a 'Native' Anthropologist?" *American Anthropologist, 95*(3), 1993: 671–686.

Panourgiá, Neni and George E. Marcus, eds. *Ethnographica Moralia: Experiments in Interpretive Anthropology.* New York: Fordman University Press, 2008.

Puar, Jasbir. "Global Circuits: Transnational Sexualities and Trinidad." *Signs, 26*(4), 2001: 1039–1065.

Rofel, Lisa. "Qualities of Desire: Imagining Gay Identities in China." *GLQ, 5*(4), 1999: 451–474.

Rosaldo, Renato. *Culture and Truth: The Remaking of Social Analysis.* Boston: Beacon Press, 1993.

Rust, Paula C. "The Politics of Sexual Identity: Sexual Attraction and Behavior among Lesbian and Bisexual Women." *Social Problems, 39*(4), 1992: 366–386.

Stacey, Judith. "Can There Be a Feminist Ethnography?" *Women's Studies International Forum, 11*(1), 1988: 21–27.

Stanley, Liz and Sue Wise. *Breaking Out: Feminist Consciousness and Feminist Research.* London: Routledge and Kegan Paul, 1983.

Stein, Arlene. *Sex and Sensibility: Stories of a Lesbian Generation.* Berkeley: University of California Press, 1997.

Strathern, Marilyn. "An Awkward Relationship: The Case of Feminism and Anthropology." *Signs, 12*(2), 1987: 276–292.

Taussig, Michael. *The Devil and Commodity Fetishism in South America.* Chapel Hill: University of North Carolina Press, 1983.

Venkatesh, Sudhir. *Off the Books: The Underground Economy of the Urban Poor.* Cambridge, MA: Harvard University Press, 2006.

Wacquant, Loïc. *Body and Soul: Notebooks of an Apprentice Boxer.* New York: Oxford University Press, 2004.

Walker, Lisa. "How to Recognize a Lesbian: The Cultural Politics of Looking Like What You Are." *Signs, 18*(4), 1993: 866–890.

Ware, Vron and Les Back. *Out of Whiteness: Color, Politics, and Culture.* Chicago: University of Chicago Press, 2001.

Weston, Kath. *Gender in Real Time: Power and Transience in a Visual Age.* New York: Routledge, 2002.

––––––––––. *Long Slow Burn: Sexuality and Social Science.* New York: Routledge, 1998.

Queer in the Field: On Emotions, Temporality, and Performativity in Ethnography

ALISON ROOKE

This article is a reflection on a year of ethnographic fieldwork conducted in and around a lesbian and gay community center in London. The research was concerned with the ways in which working class lesbian and bisexual women experience the meanings of their sexual identities on an everyday basis. I conducted participant observation in a variety of settings. Activities I took part in included volunteering at the center and running sexualities discussion groups, and photographic workshops with lesbian and bisexual women. In this article I explore the epistemological, ontological, and ethical dimensions of ethnographic research. I argue here that queer ethnography is not merely ethnography that has focus on researching queer lives, it is also a matter of taking queer theory seriously in order to question the conventions of ethnographic research, specifically the stability and coherence of the ethnographic self and performativity of the ethnographic self in writing and doing research. To queer ethnography then, is to bend the established orientation of ethnography in its method, ethics, and reflexive philosophical principles.

INTRODUCTION

This article is a reflection on a year of ethnographic fieldwork conducted in and around a lesbian and gay community center in London. The research was concerned with the ways in which working-class lesbian and bisexual women experience the meanings of their sexual identities on an everyday basis. I conducted participant observation in a variety of settings. Activities I took part in included volunteering at the center and running sexualities discussion groups, and photographic workshops with lesbian and bisexual women. In this article I explore the epistemological, ontological, and ethical dimensions of ethnographic research. I argue here that queer ethnography is not merely ethnography that focuses on researching queer lives; it is also a matter of taking queer theory seriously in order to question the conventions of ethnographic research, specifically the stability and coherence of the ethnographic self and the performativity of this self in writing and doing research. To *queer* ethnography then, is to bend the established orientation of ethnography in its method, ethics, and reflexive philosophical principles.

Ethnographic research methodologies have received considerable criticism (much of this coming from ethnographers themselves), regarding the conditions of historical emergence, being born out of the inequalities of modernity, and institutionalized within Western colonialism. Following the postmodern turn in anthropology (Clifford and Marcus, 1986; Geertz, 1973; Marcus, 1986; Clifford, 1986, 1988, 1997), the conditions of ethnographic knowledge production, and modes of representation, have been passionately debated.[1] Issues such as the ethnographer's positionality, the possibilities and limitations of knowing and understanding, the method's lack of "scientificity," its potentially exploitative nature, its historical production of the colonial "Other," the perils of representation, and the relationship between theory and practice have all been interrogated with rigor. Ethnography is a discipline that is undoubtedly methodologically untidy, and university bookshelves are filled with some of the anxious writing that this messy methodology seems to produce. And yet, rather than meekly apologizing for its sins and leaving the room quietly, ethnography has proliferated and flourished as both a method of research and as mode of representation.[2] Today ethnography, at its best, continues to be a genre of sociological and anthropological writing that has the power to richly communicate the irreducibility of human experience in a time when the hunger for "human stories," whether on "reality" TV or in the form of confessional novels, seems to be endless. One mark of the skillful ethnographic scholar is an ability to witness and record the lived complexity of the social world. The best ethnographies write about this in a way that, rather than merely offering potentially poetic, up-close accounts of lived experience, produce analyses that offer a concrete sense of the social world, which is at once "internally sprung and dialectically produced" (Willis and Trondman, 2000), communicating something about the ways in which our private and public lives are caught in the flow of history, the discourses that surround us, and the webs of meaning we weave ourselves.

In carrying out queer ethnographic research into lesbian lives, my aim was to offer an account that interrogates the everyday dimensions of lived experience and describes workings of heteronormativity, homonormativity, and their consequences. I was particularly interested in how women live in relationship to the meanings of the category "lesbian" and wanted to analyze the ways in which the changing meanings of the identity category "lesbian" are discursively produced in sociohistorical context. Queer, postmodern, and poststructural theories of knowledge production and the self, combined with a commitment to ethnographic understanding, offer a productive space of praxis in which we can think through the "necessary trouble" (Butler, 1991) of identity categories, theorize the complexity of the ways in which contemporary sexual subjectivities are discursively produced while simultaneously doing justice to the ways in which identities, such as lesbian, are lived with intersubjective complexity.

THE QUEER ETHNOGRAPHER

> Let's face it. We're undone by each other. And if we're not, we're missing something. (Butler, 2003: 31)
> [I]f you want to understand what a science is, you should look in the first instance not at its theories or its findings, and certainly not at what its apologists say about it; you should look at what the practitioners of it do. (Geertz, 1973: 5)

Butler's statement, which opens this section, points toward an ethic and ontology of vulnerability, of how our sense of self is made through the inevitability of loss, and the ways in which we are connected and indebted to each other. When researching the social world qualitatively, these connections also exist within our research encounters. Gathering ethnographic "data" depends on haptic human connection, closeness, understanding, and personal engagement. This affective process requires a sensory involvement that, in an attempt to convey and make some sense of embodied experience, takes emotions and feelings seriously. This ethic of connection is often at odds with the kind of distanced, rational and reasoned theoretical texts ethnographers produce in a discipline that prioritizes distance, reflection, and abstraction.[3] This is captured beautifully by Ruth Behar when discussing her experience of moving from research to writing.

> Loss, mourning, the longing for memory, the desire to enter into the world around you and having no idea how to do it, the fear of observing too coldly or too distractedly or too raggedly, the rage of cowardice, the insight that is always arriving too late, as defiant hindsight, a sense of the utter uselessness of writing anything and yet the burning desire to write something are the stopping places along the way. (Behar, 1996: 3)

Throughout the fieldwork period I found myself continually caught between intense phatic engagement (participation) and a kind of cool intellectual detachment (observation). I felt a deep unease when attempting to retain some objectivity and keep my feelings to myself while trying to engage and understand my informants' experiences through an ethic of listening that combines the emotions and the intellect, in what Bourdieu (1999) describes as "intellectual love."[4] In order to establish these connections the ethnographer must have a degree of emotional competence, and an ability to convey genuine interest, express care, and respond appropriately with the desired outcome of establishing feelings of trust in mind. This is sometimes glibly described as "establishing rapport" in classic anthropology texts. It is on the basis of this emotional labor (Hochschild, 1983),[5] which produces bonds of trust, that informants "open up" to give clear accounts of themselves. Furthermore, the self-explanations offered to the ethnographer are offered on the basis of the informants understanding of the *kind of person* the ethnographer is. Rather than inhabit the position of "modest witness" (Haraway, 1996) I presented myself with honesty as a White working-class lesbian and a researcher. It was, in part, due to my embodied situatedness in these subject positions and my communicating some shared understanding of the pleasures and difficulties of lesbian lives, that informants were willing to disclose their life experiences and self understandings to me. If then, the "field" is intersubjectively constructed by the ethnographer, we might argue that he or she is the *only* person who inhabits the field *as* "the field." The informants may be in the same place at the same time but their experience of it is different to that of the ethnographer. This is precisely the challenge of ethnographic scholarship and is illustrated beautifully in the following passage by John Berger:

> What separates us from the characters about whom we write is not knowledge, either objective or subjective, but their experience of time in the story we are telling. This separation allows us, the storytellers, the power of knowing the whole. Yet equally, this separation renders us powerless: we cannot control our characters after the narration has begun. ... The time and therefore the story belongs to them, yet the meaning of the story, what makes it worthy of being told is what we can see and what inspires us because we are beyond its time. ... Those who read or listen to our stories see everything as through a lens. His lens is the secret of narration, and it is ground anew in every story, ground between the temporal and the timeless. (Berger, 1991: 31)

The people we write about, those whose stories we aim to tell, embody and live in their own time and their stories go on long after we have left the "field." The ethnographer's challenge is to grapple with the meaning of the story, to tell it with honesty and an ethical commitment to doing it justice.

It is not so much that the ethnographer is armed with a theoretical and methodological toolbox, possessing a superior "objective" knowledge. Indeed, ethnographic knowledge is "partial, committed and incomplete" (Clifford, 1986: 7) but this partiality is not a strength, not a flaw; it is a way of acknowledging our social and political situatedness as researchers.[6]

Although the emotional aspects of carrying out ethnographic research have often been selectively written out of accounts of the ethnography the erotic dimension of fieldwork has suffered an even more striking silence. While sociologists and anthropologists have been fascinated with the sexual and intimate lives of others, they have been particularly silent about their own erotic subjectivity. As Kulick points out, this has been due to anthropology's "disciplinary distain for personal narratives" and cultural taboos about discussing their own cultures sex, while constructing the often "exotic sexualities of others" (1995: 20). Crucially, this works to maintain the bounded subjectivity of the (usually male) ethnographer and the limits of legitimate critical enquiry while simultaneously silencing women and gays.[7] As Newton points out, (Newton, 2000) this silence works to keep heterosexual male subjectivity out of the lens of critical enquiry. By "writing out," rather than "writing up" the erotic equation in fieldwork, sexuality continues to be the dirty secret kept in the epistemological closet of research ethics. Paying attention to the work of emotions and exotics in ethnography, as part of a feminist and reflexive ethnographic project, is, in part, an impetus to question the way in which the ontological and epistemological boundary between the "knower" and the "known" is produced and maintained in the discursive production of "us" and "them." In this spirit Marcus suggests that "the ethnographer's framework should not remain intact if the subject's subjectivity is being analytically pulled apart" (Marcus, 1994: 50).

I want to suggest here that queering ethnography requires that we make apparent the normative logics of ethnographic practice and that we undo some textual conventions that construct the ethnographers' gendered and sexual subjectivity as unproblematically stable. We might ask ourselves, as ethnographers of queer lives, while we are busy deconstructing the discourses and categories that produce our informants subjectivities, to what extent are we willing to be "pulled apart" or undone? Are we willing to risk relinquishing our often unspoken attachment to the categories that offer us a sense of ontological security? To illustrate, at the start of my fieldwork, I had a feminist ethical commitment to collaboration and dialogue (Skeggs, 1997; Stacey, 1988; Stanley and Wise, 1983a, 1983b, 1990, 1993) that I assumed would prove relatively unproblematic to put into practice. My undeclared attachment to ethnographic distance and the comfort and authority it offers was repeatedly made obvious to me while carrying out my fieldwork. So, for example, one of my "informants" turned out to be friends with one of my former lovers and went on to make it clear that she knew some of the details of our break-up. I realized I was happy to be known in some ways but not in others. Carrying out fieldwork was a space where my personal boundaries and my stable sense of my self were gradually undone. This is best summed up in Geertz's assertion that "You don't exactly penetrate another culture, as the masculinist image would have it. You put yourself in its way and it bodies forth and enmeshes you" (Geertz, 1995). This gendered and sexualized metaphor draws attention to the sexual subjectivity of the ethnographer, a matter that continues to be surrounded by a slightly embarrassed, uneasy silence. While queer theory has decentered and fragmented the research "subject's" subjectivities, the self that is producing much cultural research remains somewhat distant and stable. So for example, much anthropological reflexive writing has at its center a somewhat disconnected self that is bounded, integral, and stable through space and time. As Willson points out:

> Many ethnographers go to the field with the illusion that their identity, like their body, is discrete and impenetrable, that although their public persona is controllable and flexible, they have an inner identity, a kind of holy ground like a silent pool of water that nothing will touch. (Willson, 1995: 256)

Perhaps as a way of countering this tendency, Probyn asks "just what exactly a self-reflecting self is reflecting upon?" (1993: 80), suggesting that the reflexive self should be "both an object of enquiry and the means of analyzing where and how the self is lodged within the social formation" (Probyn 1993: 80). I want to argue here, that an intellectual commitment to queer theory *and* queer methodology requires an epistemological openness and attention to one's own sexual subjectivity and the performativity of the self in the research process. It demands that the ethnographer work from an honest sense of oneself that is open and reflexive, rather than ontologically holding on to a sense of self that provides a stable place to enter into the fieldworld and subsequently leave from. This queer reflexivity offers a means of theoretical maneuvering by exploring the connection between ontology and epistemology. Like emotions, the peformativity of erotics in the field is a potentially useful source of reflection and knowledgemaking.

Queer reflexivity requires drawing attention to the erotics of knowledge production. Doing fieldwork, which had at its center the issue of lesbian selfhood and spatiality, was a space of reflection on my own investment in a certain version of lesbian identity. I was in, and of, the culture I was writing about. The extent to which I could establish relationships with informants affected what I could research and the limits of my study. My access to the lesbian, gay, bisexual, and transgender (LGBT) center was negotiated through my cultural and social capital. I had friends who had worked or volunteered there in the past and also knew some of the workers, a little, socially. Although I was a "cultural insider," inhabiting the ethnographic imagination often left me feeling like an outsider looking in. I was self-conscious of my performance of my lesbian credentials and the ways that my participation in discussions of sexuality and sex, my camp sensibility and bawdy sense of humor demonstrated a certain ontological security. These conscious repetitive performative displays of my lesbian cultural capital (Rooke, 2007), which I had accumulated through years of practice in bars, clubs and at work in womens' projects in the past, contributed to my acceptance and inclusion. To illustrate, while helping out in the office, I became acutely aware of the quick repartee, casual flirtatiousness, and sexual innuendo that constituted the sexuality of the office space. The conditions of my inclusion in this space was contingent on my ability to join in on it or willingness to be the butt of jokes. My lesbian identity had been formed in a specific place and time: London in the 1980s and 1990s. At the start of the fieldwork situation, I felt that I had a stable sense of myself, the meaning of my sexual identity and a future trajectory based on that ontology. However, throughout my fieldwork experience, I was forced to examine my own presumptions and consider the extent to which my particular sense of my lesbian identity was coloring my perception of the issues coming out of the research; whether the issues of importance to me were actually relevant to the women I was engaging with. These difficulties were often guiding principles in pushing my analysis forward. They challenged my preconceptions of contemporary lesbian identity.

> [C]ould it be that the subjection that subjectivates the gay or lesbian subject in some ways continues to oppress, or oppresses most insidiously, once 'outness' is claimed? Who or what is it that is 'out', made manifest and fully disclosed, when and if I reveal myself as a lesbian? What is it that is now known, anything? (Butler, 1991: 15)
> Substantial groups of women and men under this representational regime have found that the normative category 'homosexual', or its more recent synonyms, does have a real power to organize and describe their experience of their own sexuality and identity, enough at any rate to make their self application of it (even when only tacit) worth the enormous accompanying costs. Even if only for this reason, the categorization demands respect. (Sedgwick, 1991: 83)

One of the challenges and possibilities of engaging with queer theory is the ways in which it problematizes the epistemological and ontological comfort and coherence of identity categories. As the two quotations above illustrate, the category "lesbian" is as necessary as it is problematic. The category continues to have salience and political currency, as well as the power to oppress. The performativity of my subject position as a lesbian researcher during my fieldwork had been productive. It enabled much of the connection I was seeking in the research process. Quite suddenly the security and perceived authenticity of my subject position was questioned by myself and others when, about halfway through the fieldwork process, my own subjectivity was somewhat queered when I began a relationship with a female-to-male transsexual, who was in the process of transitioning. I met this man in the research process and initially mistook him as a lesbian. Our erotic relationship flourished over discussions of lesbian, gay and queer theories, discussions of gender norms and queer communities in the course of my fieldwork.

My theoretical interest in the logics of exclusion within contemporary lesbian cultures was now felt with immediacy. These difficult changes also brought about a new basis of understanding with some participants as well as ethical dilemmas. Several months into my fieldwork, together with center staff and volunteers, I began facilitating a "sexualities discussion group" for women beginning to come to terms with their sexual desires for other women. The women attending the group were mostly working class and several of them were mothers who were either married or divorced. Each week in group discussions women struggled with the stigma they associated with lesbian identities. In this space I found myself experiencing a fresh sense of empathy. In group discussions I could draw on and share my past experience of coming out as a lesbian, albeit twenty years earlier; however, I now had a more immediate understanding of the anxieties of some of the women in the group. Discussions about fears of telling family and friends, worries about being misinterpreted, rejected by friends, the fear of social stigma now had more immediacy and resonance for me. I was acutely conscious of the necessity of identity and the enormous personal costs that go with identifying with the category and yet I was simultaneously aware of the ways in which identity is an unfinished narrative, that the coherence that it offers does not do justice to many queer lives which are often conflicted, contradictory, and defy the coherence of these categories. Although I knew I had a lot to offer women who were struggling with the shame and stigma of being a lesbian, I also felt my participation in the group was somewhat inauthentic. I was presenting myself as someone who was a lesbian supporting other lesbians when I no longer felt that I fitted within that category. My self-presentation began to feel increasingly like a partial, unfinished narrative. I shared experiences of my first coming out but remained silent on the second. My growing awareness of, and commitment to, trans politics meant that I was uncomfortable about being evasive about my partner's trans identity (and more generally this was not always possible due to his gender-ambiguous appearance while he was going through his transition). My situation caused me to question the status of my insider knowledge and what it *does*. Should I mention my relationship? What would I say in the group if people asked whether I was in a relationship? Should I present myself as the confident secure lesbian role model that some of these women sought? Should I confuse this apparent coherence? By writing about these dilemmas would I be indulging in "banal egotism" (Probyn, 1993: 80)? Was I merely reflecting on others in order to talk about myself? Carrying out ethnographic fieldwork brought my sexual subjectivity, and that of the informants I worked with, into sharp focus. It forced me to ask myself whether the personal cost of being on the margins of some of the more conventional understandings of lesbian identity would be too great and whether it would jeopardize my project. I began to feel more marginal and less a "cultural insider." I asked myself, what conflicts of meaning would be overlooked if I denied my ambivalent situation?

I want to argue here that the ethnographic self is as contingent, plural, and shifting as that of many of the informants we are concerned with. Paying attention to this provisionality is a matter of questioning the self at the heart of ethnographic account found in the social sciences, asking how we connect with others, the purpose of reflexivity, and the importance of honest and rigorous considerations of the vulnerability of the observer (Behar, 1996; Moreno, 1995). Reflexivity then, is not merely intellectual and epistemological "navel gazing" but rather a matter of acknowledging one's subject position in the power relations of research, and interrogating "a discursive arrangement that holds together in tensions, the different lines of race, and sexuality that form and reform our senses of self" (Probyn, 1993: 1–2). This is a "theoretically maneuvering" self rather than a stable, coherent, and impenetrable individual.

I have set out here some of the ethical, methodological, and ontological difficulties of researching the meanings of lesbian identities ethnographically with a commitment to queering some of the scholastic conventions of ethnography. The issues raised by the earlier discussion of queer ethnography—its temporality, matters of intersubjectivity, emotional labor, the limits of the queer self, and reflexivity—raise questions regarding ontological and epistemological locatedness. More broadly they ask "What kind of ethnographic imagination we should aim to embody?" I want to suggest that the "professional rite of passage" that is the ethnographic journey is not merely about stepping out of the academy and into the messy social worlds of the "field." It is also about embracing the queerness of the situations we find ourselves in, leading to an ethnography that recognizes experience as a nodal point of knowledge, providing useful information about the self, subjects, and the spaces they inform and are informed by (Probyn, 1993). My experience over the period described was one of journeying without a map, moving within and between categories, slipping out of the comfort of identities of "lesbian" and "researcher," engaging with the instability and challenges to thinking that this brings, emphasizing the importance of being able to move beyond that location, out of our mindset, theoretical orientations, and preconceptions. Queer ethnography requires doing justice to the ways that people live their sexual identities with complexity and questioning the conditions of knowledge production when theorizing queer lives.

NOTES

1. The Duneier versus Wacquant debate in the pages of the *American Journal of Sociology* (2002) being just one example.

2. Ethnography is a research method that has travelled out of the academy, being increasingly popular with corporations concerned with matters such as the ways people use technologies, for example, the Ethnographic Praxis in Industry Conference 2005 held at the Microsoft Campus Seattle Washington.

3. Both ethnographic and feminist debates regarding research methodologies have opened up a space for challenging the model of the rational detached researcher who maintains critical distance from his or her subjects (Code, 1991, 1993; Haraway, 1988; Harding and Hintikka, 1983; Skeggs, 1994; Stacey, 1988; Stanley, 1990; Stanley and Wise, 1983a, 1983b, 1990, 1993).

4. Bourdieu's ethical listening aims to offer the research subject an opportunity "to testify, make themselves heard, carry their experience over from the private to the public sphere; an opportunity also to explain them in the fullest sense of the word" (Bourdieu, 1999: 612–615). The encounter with the researcher, when conducted with the ethic that Bourdieu suggests, can offer up a unique opportunity for self-examination. This is not without its problems (see McRobbie's (2002) critique of *The Weight of the World* and the limits of Bourdieu's project of "social pedagogy").

5. Although much ethnographic writing has focused on emotions as culturally variant constructions—legitimate and important forms of understanding for both informants and ethnographers (see Rosaldo, 1989; Coffey, 1999) I am arguing that little writing on the emotions of ethnographic field-work acknowledges the extent to which ethnography is a form of emotional labor with its own hazards and difficulties and gendered dimensions.

6. There is an often-unacknowledged overlap between postmodern ethnography and feminist critiques of research methodologies. Both reject the stance of the natural observer, recognize the intrusive and unequal nature of research relationships in the field, are self conscious of the potential for distortion and the limitations of the research process, and both recognize that they are producing "partial truths."

7. For more discussion and examples of ethnographic texts that do interrogate these matters see Kulick and Willson (1995) and Newton (2000).

REFERENCES

Behar, Ruth. *The Vulnerable Observer: Anthropology That Breaks Your Heart*. Boston: Beacon Press, 1996.

Berger, J. *And Our Faces, My Heart, Brief as Photos*: New York: Vintage International, 1991.

Bourdieu, P., et al *The Weight of the World—Social Suffering in Contemporary Society*. Cambridge: Polity Press, 1999.

Butler, J. "Imitation and Gender Insubordination." In D. Fuss, ed. *Inside/Out: Lesbian Theories, Gay Theories*. London: Routledge, 1991: 13–31.

———. *Precarious Life: Powers of Mourning and Violence*. London: Verso, 2003.

Clifford, J. and G. Marcus. *Writing Culture: The Politics and Poetics of Ethnography*. Berkeley: University of California Press, 1986.

———. *The Predicament of Culture: Twentieth-Century Ethnography, Literature and Art*. Cambridge, MA: Harvard University Press, 1988.

———. *Routes: Travel and Translation in the Late Twentieth Century*. Cambridge, MA: Harvard University Press, 1997.

Code, L. *What Can She Know? Feminist Theory and the Construction of Knowledge*. Ithaca and London: Cornell University Press, 1991.

———. "Feminist Epistemology." In Jonathan Dancy and Ernest Sosa, eds. *A Companion to Epistemology*. Oxford and Cambridge, MA: Blackwell, 1993.

Coffey, A. *The Ethnographic Self—Fieldwork and the Representation of Identity.* London: Sage, 1999.

Duneier, M. (2002) "What Kind of Combat Sport is Sociology?" *American Journal of Sociology, 107*(6), 2002: 1551–1576.

Geertz, C. *The Interpretation of Culture.* New York: Basic Books, 1973.

———. "The Uses of Diversity." In B. Robert, ed. *Assessing Cultural Anthropology.* USA: McGraw Hill, 1994: 454–467.

———. *After the Fact: Two Countries, Four Decades, One Anthropologist.* Cambridge, MA: Harvard University Press, 1995.

Haraway, D. "Situated Knowledges: The Science Question in Feminism and the Privilege of Partial Perspective." *Feminist Studies, 14*(3). 1988: 575–599.

———. *Modest_Witness@Second_Millennium. FemaleMan_Meets_OncoMouse: Feminism and Technoscience.* New York: Routledge, 1996.

Harding, K. and M. Hintikka, eds. *Discovering Reality: Feminist Perspectives on Epistemology, Metaphysics, Methodology, and Philosophy of Science.* London: Reidel Publishing, 1983.

Hochschild, A. R. *The Managed Heart: Commercialisation of Human Feeling.* London: UCL Press, 1983.

Kulick, D. "The Sexual Life of the Anthropologist: Erotic Subjectivity and Ethnographic Work." In Don Kulick and Margaret Willson, eds. *Taboo. Sex, Identity and Erotic Subjectivity in Anthropological Fieldwork.* Routledge: London, 1995.

Kulick, D. and M. Willson. *Taboo. Sex, Identity and Erotic Subjectivity in Anthropological Fieldwork.* London: Routledge, 1995.

Marcus, G. E. "Contemporary Problems of Ethnography in the Modern World System." In J. Clifford and G. E. Marcus, eds. *Writing Culture: The Politics and Poetics of Ethnography.* Berkeley: University of California Press, 1986.

———. "After the Critique of Ethnography: Faith, Hope and Charity, but the Greatest of These is Charity." In B. Robert ed. *Assessing Cultural Anthropology.* New York: McGraw Hill Inc., 1994: 40–55.

McRobbie, A. "A Mixed Bag Of Misfortunes." *Theory Culture and Society, 19,* 2002: 192.

Moreno, E. "Rape in the Field, Reflections for a Survivor." In Don Kulick and Margaret Willson, eds. *Taboo. Sex, Identity and Erotic Subjectivity in Anthropological Fieldwork.* London: Routledge, 1995: 219–250.

Newton, E. *Margaret Mead Made Me Gay: Personal Essays, Public Ideas.* Durham, NC: Duke, 2000.

Probyn, E. *Sexing the Self: Gendered Positions in Cultural Studies.* London: Routledge, 1993.

Rooke, A. "Navigating Embodied Lesbian Space: Towards a Lesbian Habitus." *Space and Culture, 10,* 2007: 231.

Rosaldo, R. *Culture and Truth: The Remaking of Social Analysis.* Boston: Beacon, 1989.

Sedgwick, E. K. *The Epistemology of the Closet.* London: Harvester Wheatsheaf, 1991.

Stacey, J. "Can There be a Feminist Ethnography?" *Women's Studies International Forum, 11,* 1988: 21–27.

Stanley, L., ed. *Feminist Praxis: Research, Theory and Epistemology in Feminist Sociology.* London: Routledge, 1990.

———— and S. Wise. "Back into the Personal or: Our Attempt to Construct 'Feminist Research.'" In G. Bowles and R. D. Klein, eds. *Theories of Women's Studies*. London: Routledge, 1983a: 192–209.

———— and S. Wise. *Breaking Out: Feminist Consciousness and Feminist Research*. London: Routledge and Kegan Paul, 1983b.

———— and S. Wise "Method, Methodology and Epistemology in Feminist Research Processes." In L. Stanley, ed. *Feminist Praxis: Research, Theory and Epistemology in Feminist Sociology*. London: Routledge, 1990.

———— and S. Wise. *Breaking Out Again: Feminist Ontology and Epistemology*. London: Routledge, 1993.

Skeggs, B. "Situating the Production of Feminist Ethnography." In M. Maynard and J. Purvis eds. London: Taylor and Francis, 1994: 72–93.

————. *Formations of Class and Gender—Becoming Respectable*. London: Sage, 1997.

Willson, M. (1995). "Perspective and Difference: Sexualisation, the Field and the Ethnographer." In Don Kulick and Margaret Willson, eds. *Taboo. Sex, Identity and Erotic Subjectivity in Anthropological Fieldwork*. London: Routledge, 1995: 251–275.

Willis, P. and M. Trondman (2000). "Manifesto for Ethnography." *Ethnography*, *1*(1), 2000: 5–16.

Wacquant, L. (2002). "Scrutinizing the Street: Poverty, Morality, and the Pitfalls of Urban Ethnography." *American Journal of Sociology*, *107*(6), 2002: 1468–1532.

Researching Domestic Violence in Same-Sex Relationships—A Feminist Epistemological Approach to Survey Development

MARIANNE HESTER

CATHERINE DONOVAN

The article draws on recently completed research by the authors, involving a detailed study of love and intimate partner violence in same-sex and heterosexual relationships (funded by the ESRC, award RES-000-23-0650). The research, hitherto the most detailed study of its kind in the United Kingdom, included a national same- sex community survey (n = 800) plus four focus groups and interviews with 67 individuals identifying as lesbian, gay, queer, bisexual, transgender, or heterosexual. The article discusses in particular the development of the same-sex community survey, focusing on the epistemological and methodological implications of using a feminist approach.

BACKGROUND

Domestic violence in heterosexual relationships began to be identified from the late 1960s, with the U.K. women's movement at the forefront of developing support and services. In the wake of these activities an extensive literature and research on heterosexual domestic violence now exists in both the United Kingdom and internationally (Hester et al., 2007; Hester, 2004). Research on domestic violence in same-sex relationships has a much more recent history. During the 1980s and 1990s there was some discussion, in the

United Kingdom and elsewhere, about domestic violence in lesbian relationships and to a lesser extent gay male relationships, and how such behavior might be tackled. At the same time, there were strong tendencies to minimize, hide, and deny the existence of such abuse. A number of factors may be seen to have contributed to the greater invisibility of same-sex domestic abuse, including fears of making obvious such problems within communities already considered "problematic" in a homophobic society, and contexts where conservative governments were attempting to re-impose "traditional family values."

The early literature and studies on same-sex domestic violence was focused mainly on lesbians. Lesbians were becoming visible as a domestic violence "group," beginning to access domestic violence or rape support services ostensibly set up for heterosexual women or seeking help via lesbian or gay community organizations (Lobel, 1986). Studies on domestic violence in gay male relationships have emerged much more recently, building on concerns about and studies on gay men's health (Island and Letellier, 1991).

While studies on domestic violence in lesbian relationships have included both interview samples as well as surveys, studies of domestic violence in gay male relationships have tended to be more survey based and to build on health-related questionnaires (McClennen, 2005). Few studies directly compare lesbian and gay male domestic abuse, or attempt to compare abuse in same-sex and heterosexual relationships (e.g., Turrell, 2000; Tjaden and Thoennes, 2000). In the United Kingdom specifically, there has been only a small number of local and national surveys and qualitative research exploring same-sex domestic violence and use of services (e.g., Henderson, 2003).

Studies from the United States increasingly suggest that prevalence of domestic violence may be similar across same-sex and heterosexual relationships, and what differs are help-seeking behaviors (McClennen, 2005). However, it is not possible to achieve random, representative samples of those in same-sex relationships and comparisons between studies on same-sex domestic violence are difficult because of the use of a variety of methodologies and samples, and varying definitions of violence and abuse. Consequently, rates of prevalence have tended to vary enormously across the studies.

FRAMING THE RESEARCH

Feminist scholarship has developed "gender and power" analyses of domestic violence that problematize the social construction of masculinity as embodied in heterosexual men, explaining domestic violence as the exertion of power and control by men over women in intimate relationships within contexts of gender inequality (Hester, 2004). There is currently a debate about the extent to which this explanatory model can be applied to domestic violence in same-sex relationships. Renzetti (1992), for instance, in research on domestic violence in lesbian relationships, argues that a gender and power analysis can be applied, but needs to be expanded to take into account the different experiences, meanings, and interventions related to domestic violence that "intersectionality" provides. That is, not just gender, but also the effects of location and discrimination linked to sexuality, race, and ethnicity. Ristock (2003) is more critical of the gender and power framework, seeing this as providing a heterosexual bias and wanting to focus on the specific experiences of lesbian domestic violence, while acknowledging the need to retain "a necessary analysis of the pervasiveness of male violence against women" (p. 20). She argues that in lesbian relationships experiences of domestic violence are heterogenous and social context is particularly important, with a lack of binary categories such as "victim" and "perpetrator." By contrast, Island and Letellier (1991), focusing on gay men, argue that a "gender and power" model does not apply at all to same-sex domestic violence and instead suggest that gender-neutral and individual, psychological models should be applied. These debates led us to want to explore how processes of gendering and power might operate in similar or different ways in abusive lesbian, gay male, or heterosexual relationships. It has also been argued that violence in same-sex relationships are characterized by bi-directional "common couple" or "situational" violence, by contrast to heterosexual relationships where uni-directional "patriarchal or intimate terrorism" is more prominent (Johnson, 2006). Consequently we wanted to explore experiences of abuse from partners as well as their own use of such behavior.

Thus, it was important that we adopt a general approach that could deal with issues of context, gender, power, and sexuality, let alone other differences. We adopted a feminist epistemological approach as this would help us to construct research instruments geared to exploring how processes of gendering and power might operate in similar or different ways in abusive lesbian, gay male, or heterosexual relationships. The survey instrument also needed to provide data regarding a range of domestically abusive behavior while taking into account both context and impact, and to include questions about experiences of abuse from partners and use of such behavior against partners.

A FEMINIST EPISTEMOLOGICAL APPROACH

To think epistemologically is to ask questions about what can be known, and the interrelationship between knowledge, experience, and "reality" (Skinner, Hester, and Malos, 2005). However, how knowledge, experience, and reality might interrelate is an area of contestation within feminist debates

(Ramazanoğlu with Holland, 2002). There can be different epistemologies and they lead to different knowledge about the social world.

For us, the importance of adopting a feminist epistemological approach is that such approaches have a questioning of power, gender, and sexuality as a central focus. The relationship between gender and power is of course something that is not straightforward, and is indeed contested among feminists—resulting in, for instance, "standpoint" or "postmodern" approaches with distinctions between how to understand reality and who are the knowers. "Standpoint" approaches seek to understand the experience of oppression from the positioning as subordinated, where women or lesbians and gay men may all be constituted as the "ruled" (Smith, 1988). Postmodern approaches instead attempt to understand the many "realities" and subjugated knowledges discoursively produced at different times and locations, tending also to a rejection of "static" identity positions such as "women," "lesbian," and "gay men."

Our approach draws from both these traditions but with an emphasis on the material and on the constructions and experiences related to structural oppressions. Domestic violence is not merely "discursive," it is experienced materially and bodily, although its impact is situated in relation to time and space (Hester, 2004). The impact of domestic violence may vary between individuals due to their location in particular sets of social relations and different contexts. For instance, the impact of domestic violence on heterosexual men may be less severe than the impact on heterosexual women (Walby and Allen, 2004), while the experiences of lesbians living in abusive relationships may be more heterogenous than those of heterosexual women (Ristock, 2002). Such an approach also takes into account the intersecting of potential inequalities or differences such as those associated with gender, sexuality, race, ethnicity, age, disability, and class (Crenshaw, 1989, and as indicated in relation to the work of Renzetti, 1992).

HOW DO WE KNOW AND HOW DO WE FIND OUT?

Understanding how gender and sexuality intersect with regard to how individuals may use, experience, and embody domestic violence are crucial to our project of comparing similarities and differences across abusive lesbian, gay male, or heterosexual relationships. Also, we see knowledge about domestic violence—what it is, what it does—as rooted in the accounts of survivors, and to a lesser extent in the accounts of perpetrators of domestic violence and witnesses (Hester et al., 2007). The use of "experience" in feminist research is of course an area of contestation (Ramazanoğlu with Holland, 2002). We do not see experience as providing "truth," that is, accounts of experiences are "stories" that may vary in their telling over time and to different audiences. Nonetheless, how individuals report experience does help us to begin to understand similarities and differences across heterosexual and lesbian and gay lives, to develop our understanding of the questions that need to be asked, and thus to construct better research instruments that reflect situated knowledge. As Ramazanoğlu with Holland (2002) point out "[d]espite the problematic status of accounts of experience, they provide knowledge that otherwise does not exist" (p. 127). However, there is much more research on this in heterosexual than in lesbian relationships, and even fewer studies involving the detailed accounts of gay men.

The obvious approach would thus have been to further develop knowledge of intimate relationships that might be abusive, via in-depth interviews with a range of lesbians, gay men, and heterosexuals. We did indeed adopt such an approach, and carried out in-depth interviews with 19 individuals identifying as lesbian, 19 as gay men, 23 as heterosexual, 3 as bisexual, and 3 as queer (Donovan and Hester, 2007). However, we also wanted to apply the same epistemological approach in the development of a questionnaire survey that would reach a much wider sample of individuals in same-sex relationships, and which could be used to compare data on domestic violence among individuals identifying as lesbian, gay, bisexual, and transgender (LGBT) or queer (Q) with those identifying as heterosexual. We therefore set out to develop a questionnaire that would not only draw on existing surveys of domestic violence, such as the British Crime Survey, but would incorporate questions that might reflect to a greater extent "how we know" about such violence in same sex as well as in heterosexual relationships. In other words, to reflect what previous research on "experience" of domestic violence tells us about the possible features and dynamics of such abuse, while at the same time allowing new knowledge to emerge.

The way domestic violence is given meaning or is defined has changed over time and in relation to different contexts and actors (Hester, 2004). Based largely on heterosexual women's experiences, but also echoed by interviews with individuals in same-sex relationships, domestic violence has since the 1970 s tended to be seen by feminists as ongoing patterns of coercive control, or "power-over," involving a variety of violent and abusive behaviors, whether physical, sexual, and/or emotional (Hester et al., 2007; Renzetti, 1992). At the same time there may also be distinctions between situations involving coercive control, and bi-directional or "situational" violence (Johnson, 2006; Ristock, 2002). However, it can be difficult using questionnaires to capture "patterns over time," to identify what individuals may experience as "coercive control" or "situational" violence, let alone to take into account different contexts for the abuse. In what follows we discuss some of the ways in which we attempted to address these issues in constructing the questionnaire.

It should be noted that not all aspects of the questionnaire are discussed here. For a detailed outline of the contents and sampling see McCarry et al. (2008). The questionnaire included sections on: personal demographic information; decision making and conflict resolution in own relationship; own experience of negative emotional/physical/sexual behaviors including impact; own use of negative emotional/physical/sexual behaviors against partner including why this happened; help-seeking; and a final section asking whether the respondent had experienced domestic abuse plus other questions eliciting views and opinions.

TO NAME OR NOT TO NAME SOMETHING AS DOMESTIC VIOLENCE

Previous studies such as the British Crime Survey have sought to obtain levels of prevalence and incidence of domestic violence using general population samples, while others have focused more exclusively on samples of individuals already identifying as having experienced domestic violence (e.g., Renzetti, 1992). Although it is not possible to obtain a random sample of individuals identifying as LBGT&Q, we nonetheless wanted to obtain a general picture of incidence, if not prevalence, and thus sought a wide ranging, national, sample (McCarry et al., 2008).

In developing the questionnaire we were immediately faced with an important question—whether or not to name as "domestic violence" the phenomenon we were ostensibly studying. Should we be up-front in stating that this was a questionnaire about domestic violence? Or develop a questionnaire about something less obviously defined such as "problems in relationships"? Previous research has indicated the difficulties (even greater than in heterosexual relationships) involved in naming as "domestic violence" harmful or abusive behaviors or experiences within lesbian or gay male relationships (e.g., Giorgio, 2002). It might also be difficult for individuals to perceive anything other than physical violence as "domestic violence." Ethics are an important feature in feminist research (Skinner et al., 2005) and the ethics involved in using a covert or an overt approach therefore also had to be considered. We decided to carry out an extensive consultation exercise, with a range of LGBT&Q groups, newsletters, and individuals, to test which approach to use and why. Two alternative cover sheets were produced, both introducing the research as "Same-sex relationships: when things go wrong." One used the following sentence as part of the more detailed description for the research: "Recently, in the UK, there has been a growing concern to make services more relevant, appropriate and accessible to people in same sex relationships who might need help or advice because of domestic abuse." The other, using mostly the same sentence, omitted the last part: "because of domestic abuse." The majority of those consulted said they would prefer the latter, framing the questionnaire in terms of relationships generally, rather than explicitly stating a focus on domestic violence:

.... Personally, I think you should go covert as people who may be suffering domestic abuse might be put off filling it in. In addition, people who think that they aren't suffering domestic abuse but whose partners are exhibiting some of the behaviours listed might be more 'honest' about their answers if the questionnaire is not marketed as a domestic abuse questionnaire. (Critical Reviewer)

It was also apparent from the interviews, which were carried out once the questionnaire survey had been completed, that this approach helped to elicit a wider range of responses. For instance, one lesbian interviewee talked about controlling experiences she had had, not being able to get her partner to leave the house, being continually questioned about everything she did and about who she was with. She had wondered if this was adequate as the basis for saying on the questionnaire that she had experienced domestic abuse:

And, ... when I was filling out the questionnaire ... I did think, 'well actually, is this really going to count'... but it does fall into it, I think. (Kay)

Individuals such as this might not as readily have responded to a survey explicitly about domestic violence. With regard to ethics, taking a more covert approach thus seemed justifiable in that it allowed a wider range of individuals to talk about potentially abusive relationship experiences.

There was also some limited, and contradictory, feedback from individuals who had come across the questionnaire, but had decided not to fill it in. Individuals told us that they did not respond: either because they did not think the questionnaire reflected their particular experiences of domestic violence, or because it did not reflect their experience of *not* being in violent and abusive relationships. Even so, we managed to obtain a large U.K.-wide sample, with 800 respondents that in many respects echoed the general population norms of the United Kingdom, and may have been representative of the lesbian and gay male population in some respects (McCarry et al., 2008).

MOVING BEYOND "HETERONORMATIVE" DEMOGRAPHICS

The first section of the questionnaire collected general demographic information on age, gender, ethnicity, religion, sexuality, disability, income, accommodation, education, and children. These were generally similar to the questions asked in the British Crime Survey, except in relation to gender, sexuality, and children where it was important to ensure that LGBT&Q identities and family formations were represented.

The question of "gender" was open ended to allow a range of self-definitions, such as female, male, transgender, and queer. With regard to sexuality it was important to be inclusive while obtaining useable data about domestic violence in same-sex relationships. Following piloting, eight closed potential responses were listed: Bisexual, Gay man, Gay woman, Homosexual, Lesbian, Queer, Heterosexual, and Other. The "Heterosexual" option was included to allow heterosexuals who had never had a same-sex relationship to be screened out (see also Turrell, 2000), although two respondents had had a same-sex relationship at some time. Nearly two thirds of the questionnaire respondents were women (60.5%, 451/746) and a third were men (37.5%, 280/746). Women were most likely to identify as "lesbian" (69.6%, 314/451). Men mainly identified as "gay man" (76.4%, 214/280). Nearly three times more women than men defined themselves as bisexual (10.4%, 47/451 compared to 3.9%, 11/280), or as queer (2.9%, 13/451 compared to 1.4%, 4/280). At the same time, it was apparent that individuals were using the "gender" and "sexuality" categories in different ways to express their identities. For instance, five individuals identified themselves as transgendered in relation to "gender," and as bisexual, gay woman, lesbian, queer, and "other" in relation to "sexuality." A further eleven individuals identified as "other" in relation to sexuality, with all but one identifying as female in relation to "gender." Further categories of "transgender" and "transsexual" might thus have been useful to list in the sexuality section, although this had not been obvious in the piloting stage.

Our previous work on domestic violence had indicated the importance of asking about the existence of children (e.g., Hester et al., 2007), and the possibly diverse family structures that may exist in relation to LGBT&Q communities (Weeks et al., 2001). We therefore decided to include questions that elicited basic information about children and living arrangements, which could be analyzed in relation to questions on managing relationships and negotiations and behavior within them, and with questions about negative behavior and abuse. One in six of respondents (16.1%, 120/740) parented children, with the majority of parents—more than two-thirds (70.8%, 85/120)—having all or some of these children living with them. Women identifying as lesbian were most likely to parent children (24% of lesbians), followed by individuals identifying as bisexual (19.4% of bisexuals), 13.7% of gay women, 9.5% of queer, 8.6% of homosexual, and 7.5% of those identifying as gay men. Parenting was indeed an important aspect, and women were significantly more likely than men to have their children threatened or used against them in some way as part of abusive behavior.[1]

Previous research has indicated that first same-sex relationships may provide heightened risk for domestic violence (Ristock, 2002), and questions were therefore asked if respondents were currently in a same-sex relationship and if this was their first same-sex relationship. Of those who said that they were currently in a first same-sex relationship just over a third (34%)

had experienced domestic abuse, suggesting that this was a risk factor for our sample. We also asked about length of relationships and whether they lived together with their partner or not. The vast majority of respondents (86.5%) had been in a same-sex relationship during the past 12 months, with more than two-thirds currently in such a relationship (70.5%). For about one in seven it was their first same-sex relationship (14.7%). This was similar for both women and men. There were significant differences between men and women in terms of length of relationships.[2] Men (gay men and homosexual) predominated in shorter relationships, lasting up to one year, but also in relationships lasting 2 to 5 years or more than 20 years. Women (mainly lesbian and gay women) were generally more likely to have longer relationships, lasting between 1 and 20 years.

ASKING ABOUT ABUSIVE BEHAVIOR

We needed to be able to differentiate between relationships with systematic controlling behavior and relationships in which violence and abuse may be evident but where one partner does not control the other. Therefore both the intention of the perpetrator and also the impact on the victim were important aspects. The survey consequently had to capture not only the incidence of potentially abusive behaviors, including a range of experiences, but also the meanings, intentions, and outcomes of these actions. Moreover, in order to capture possible differences related to sexuality, the experiences and behaviors highlighted by individuals identifying as LGBT or Q had to be included.

Following the British Crime Survey and echoing some of the previous surveys on abuse in lesbian and gay male relationships, the questionnaire included sections on emotional, physical and sexual behaviors from partners. Each section listed a range of possible negative behaviors such as: being isolated from friends and relatives; pushed; beaten up; had sex for the sake of a quiet life; forced into sexual activity.

General population surveys such as the British Crime Survey tend to focus on heterosexual experience. In order to move beyond the "heteronormative" we drew on previous lesbian and gay male surveys, and included questions on being "outed," being accused of not being a real gay man/lesbian, and in other ways having sexuality used as forms of abuse. Questions from surveys with gay men asking about HIV-related abuse, such as withdrawing medicines, were included with the recognition that such behavior might also be relevant to any health condition where medication is used. In the British Crime Survey questions on rape and sexual assault are based on the *Sexual Offences Act* 2003, where rape is defined as something only a man (heterosexual or gay) can commit. However, it was important in our questionnaire to incorporate the experiences of women who felt they had been raped in a lesbian relationship. Echoing debate about issues of consensual and non-consensual sexual behavior among individuals identifying as LGBT or Q, questions about breach of safer sex and safe words were also included in the questionnaire. Altogether, the questionnaire listed 27 options for negative emotional behaviors, 13 negative physical behaviors, and 9 negative sexual behaviors. Individuals were asked to "tick" as many of the behaviors as they felt applied to them.

In order to differentiate between the one-off incidents and ongoing patterns of behavior, the responses were broken down into *Never*, *Sometimes*, or *Often* (during the past 12 months or before then). In addition, respondents were asked to identify whether their responses related to the behavior of a current partner, to a previous partner, or to both.

Following each of the sections about emotional, physical, and sexual behavior, respondents were asked about the impact: "about the ways any of these behaviours may have affected you," and again asked to tick as many effects as they felt applied. This included "didn't have an impact" plus a further 26 options.

The final section of the questionnaire included a further question asking respondents whether they had "experienced domestic abuse." This made it possible to compare the incidence of potentially abusive behaviors with those who answered that they had experienced an abusive relationship.

EXPERIENCES OF RESPONDENTS

More than a third of the survey respondents (38.4%, 266/692) said that they had experienced domestic abuse at some time in a same-sex relationship, including similar proportions of women (40.1%) and men (35.2%). Although the questionnaire sample was not random, and this is therefore not a measure of prevalence, these figures nonetheless suggest that domestic abuse is an issue for a considerable number of people in same-sex relationships in the United Kingdom. An even greater number of respondents indicated that they had experienced at least one form of abusive behavior from their same-sex partners.

Echoing other studies (e.g. Ristock, 2003; Walby and Allen, 2004) emotional abuse appeared to be more widespread among the survey respondents than physical and sexual abuse. However, respondents were more likely to identify physically and sexually abusive behaviors as "domestic abuse." Self-definition was most closely identified where individuals appeared to have experienced multiple forms of abuse.

Although Ristock (2003) emphasizes the heterogeneity of domestic violence experiences in lesbian relationships, our survey data also indicated many similarities including the range of abusive behaviors experienced by gay men and lesbians and the impacts of such behavior. Even so, the differences were particularly interesting, and appear to reflect wider processes of gendering and gendered norms. Gay men were significantly more likely to use physically and sexually abusive behaviors.[3] Sexual abuse was where the greatest gender differences occurred with male respondents significantly more likely than women to be forced into sexual activity, be hurt during sex, have "safe" words or boundaries disrespected, have requests for safer sex refused, and be threatened with sexual assault. When experience of potentially abusive behaviors and impact were taken into account together sexual abuse stood out even more clearly as a risk factor for gay men.[4]

Regarding impact, lesbians were significantly more likely to be affected by emotionally and sexually abusive behavior. Lesbians were also much more likely to report that the abuse made them work harder so as "to make their partner happy" or in order "to stop making mistakes," that it had an impact on their children or their relationship with their children, or made them stop trusting people.

Previous work identified "age" as an important difference in perceptions and experiences of domestic violence and other abuse (Eriksson et al., 2005; Walby and Allen, 2004). Age was also a significant feature in our survey, and often more so than gender or sexuality. Most abusive experiences, whether emotional, physical, or sexual, were reported by those individuals under 35 years.

CONCLUSION

Using a feminist epistemological approach, rooted in understandings of experience of domestic violence, including experiences and intersections related to gender and sexuality, allowed development of a detailed survey approach that takes into account a range of abusive behaviors as well as impact, context, and abuse of partners in intimate relationships. Although much previous research on domestic violence in lesbian relationships has used qualitative approaches to get at the detailed experiences of intimate partner abuse, the current research builds on such knowledge to provide a wider and larger lesbian sample that can be compared more directly with both gay male and heterosexual reports of domestically abusive behaviors. The discussion here, of some of the data, indicates the importance of such an approach in obtaining reliable data that contributes further to our analysis of how and to which extent such behaviors are experienced similarly or differently by individuals depending on sexuality, gender, or age. The approach thus takes us a step further in analysis of domestic violence by moving beyond the generally heteronormative approaches of most surveys while also taking into account lesbian, let alone gay male and heterosexual, positionings and specificities.

NOTES

1. Significance was tested using Chi-square. Chi-square significant at $p < .01$.
2. Chi-square significant at $p = .03$.
3. Chi-square significant at $p < .05$.
4. Asking a range of questions about potentially abusive behaviors and also the impacts of such experiences allowed us to develop statistical scales taking into account both behaviors and impacts. Three separate scales relating to emotional, physical, and sexual abuse were established and were found to be reliable at $> .8$ using Cronbach's Alpha.

REFERENCES

Crenshaw, K. (1989) "Demarginalizing the Intersection of Race and Sex: A Black Feminist Critique of Antidiscrimination Doctrine, Feminist Theory, and Antiracist Politics," *University of Chicago Legal Forum*, 139–178.

Donovan, C., M. Hester, J. Holmes, and M. McCarry. (2006) Comparing domestic abuse in same sex and heterosexual relationships, initial report from ESRC study: Award No. RES-000-23-0650. Available at <http://www.bristol.ac.uk/vawrg>

Eriksson, M., M. Hester, S. Keskinen, and K. Pringle. (2005) (Eds) Tackling Men's Violence in Families – Nordic issues and dilemmas, Policy Press.

Giorgio, G. "Speaking Silence: Definitional Dialogues in Abusive Lesbian Relationships," *Violence Against Women*, 8(10), 2002: 1233–1259.

Henderson, L. *Prevalence of Domestic Violence among Lesbians and Gay Men*. London: Sigma Research, 2003.

Hester, M. "Future Trends and Developments—Violence Against Women In Europe and East Asia," *Violence Against Women*, 10(12), 2004: 1431–1448.

————,C. Pearson and N. Harwin with H. Abrahams. *Making an Impact—Children and Domestic Violence: A Reader*. 2nd ed. London: Jessica Kingsley, 2007.

Island, D., and P. Letellier. *Men Who Beat the Men Who Love Them*. New York: Harrington Park Press, 1991.

Johnson, M. P. (2006) "Conflict and Control: Gender Symmetry and Asymmetry in Domestic Violence," *Violence Against Women*, 12(11), 2006: 1003–1018.

Lobel, K., ed. *Naming the Violence: Speaking Out About Lesbian Battering*. Seattle: Seal Press, 1986.

McCarry, M., M. Hester, and C. Donovan. "Researching Same Sex Domestic Violence: Constructing a Survey Methodology," *Sociological Research Online*, 13(1), 2008. http://www.socresonline.org.uk/13/1/8.html; accessed April 3, 2009.

McClennen, J. C. (2005). "Domestic Violence Between Same-Gender Partners: Recent Findings and Future Research," *Journal of Interpersonal Violence*, 20(2), 2005: 149–154.

Ramazanoğlu, C. with J. Holland. *Feminist Methodology, Challenges and Choices*. London: Sage, 2002.

Renzetti, C. M. *Violent Betrayal: Partner Abuse in Lesbian Relationships*. Newbury Park, CA: Sage, 1992.

Ristock, J. *No More Secrets: Violence in Lesbian Relationships*. London and New York: Routledge, 2002.

Skinner, T., M. Hester, and E. Malos. *Researching Gender Violence*. Cullompton: Willan, 2005.

Smith, D. *The Everyday World as Problematic: A Feminist Sociology*. Milton Keynes: Open University Press, 1988.

Tjaden, P. and N. Thoennes. *Full Report of the Prevalence, Incidence and Consequences of Violence Against Women: Findings from the National Violence Against Women Survey*. Washington: US Department of Justice, 2000.

Turrell, S. C. "A Descriptive Analysis of Same-Sex Relationship Violence for a Diverse Sample," *Journal of Family Violence*, *15*(3), 2000: 281–293.

Walby, S. and J. Allen. *Domestic Violence, Sexual Assault and Stalking: Findings from the British Crime Survey. Home Office Research Study 276*. London: Home Office, 2004.

Weeks, J., B. Heaphy, and C. Donovan. *Same Sex Intimacies: Families of Choice and Other Life Experiments*. London: Routledge, 2001.

Producing Cosmopolitan Sexual Citizens on *The L Word*

KELLIE BURNS

CRISTYN DAVIES

Using Showtime's The L Word *as a case study, we argue that lesbian sexuality and lesbian lifestyles are produced alongside broader discourses of cosmopolitan consumer citizenship. The lesbian characters in this program are first and foremost constructed through their investments in certain neo-liberal consumer and lifestyle practices that limit the possibility of what lesbian subjectivities and/or lesbian politics can or cannot become. We offer an alternative strategy of reading lesbians in image-based media and popular culture that attends to the ways in which lesbian subjectivities are produced in a climate of neo-liberal consumer and lifestyle practices that have shifted the ways in which sexual citizens are produced. Our aim is to provide a critical framework that can be applied to other lesbian-themed television texts and to a range of other image-based visual media including film, commercial advertising, and new media.*

In an interview with the lesbian magazine *Curve*, the head writer and executive producer, Ilene Chaiken, is paraphrased as saying that the show's writers represent such a diversity of lesbian experience that "if you can't relate to chic West Coast chicks ... if the show is around long enough most lesbians will eventually see themselves." No doubt everyone will have a wish list. I would like to order up some characters with body hair, ungleaming teeth, subcutaneous fat, or shorter-than-chin-length haircuts.

> Oh, and maybe with some politics. I would like to see a lot more of Pam Grier. I hope—especially in a West Coast production—that the show's sense of race will extend beyond black and white. I would like it if not every character came equipped with a handy sexual label like bisexual Alice or the self-proclaimed male lesbian Lisa (Devon Gummersall). (Eve Kosofsky Sedgwick, 2004).

Making her representation "wish list" for Showtime's *The L Word*, Eve Kosofsky Sedgwick repositions the television viewer as an active and agentic consumer of the visual while also highlighting the limited capacity of television texts to adequately represent queer bodies and lives.[1] Sedgwick's critique of the series, which first appeared in *The Chronicle of Higher Education* (Sedgwick, 2004), was reprinted as the preface to Kim Akass' and Janet McCabe's (2006) edited collection entitled *Reading The L Word: Outing Contemporary Television*. The collection offers a range of critical commentaries about how lesbian embodiment, sexuality, lifestyle, community, and politics are represented in the first two seasons of the show.

Reading The L Word is part of a growing body of scholarly work concerned with how lesbians are represented on television (Becker, 2004; Beirne, 2006, 2007; Doty, 1993, 2000; Dow, 2008; Hart, 1994; Mayne, 2000), in film (Benshoff & Griffin, 2006; Doty, 2000; Kabir, 1998; Patton, 1995; Rich, 2004; Stacey, 1995; Weiss, 1992; Whatling, 1997; White, 1999), and in other visual mediums such as commercial advertising (Chasin, 2000; Sender, 2003, 2004). Much of this work struggles, as Sedgwick's commentary does, around the capacity of lesbian representations in queer and/or mainstream popular cultural texts to adequately depict the diversity of "real" lesbian lives.

Critiques of lesbian image-based texts that are concerned with questions of representation perform the important task of problematizing the narrow portrayal of lesbians in visual culture. Their focus is primarily on dissecting the substance of the image text, asking what it *is* or *is not*. The emphasis is on evaluating the quality or effectiveness of the image text against a series of predetermined binaries: good/bad, effective/ineffective, realistic/unrealistic, political/apolitical, queer/straight. Samuel Chambers (2006), in his contribution to *Reading The L Word*, suggests that television scholars need to move beyond arguments about representation. For Chambers television does more than simply "represent" real bodies and lives; it functions as a normalising apparatus that "produces and reproduces the norms of gender and sexuality that *are* our lived reality (both physical and social)" (p. 85). Chambers' critique marks a methodological shift away from asking questions about what lesbian television texts *are* or *are not*, and toward questions of what television representations of lesbians *do*—what they produce, consume, normalize, or curtail.

Like Chambers, we are concerned in this article with what lesbian television *does*. We do not view television as an object or technology on which reality is played out, nor do we see "reality" as a fixed or stable assemblage of materialities. Instead, television is an active cultural object that produces and governs social norms and "the real" is always shaped and reshaped as social norms are contested and negotiated. Furthermore, television texts are not limited to what transpires "on screen" within a particular programming time slot. We maintain that related websites, gossip magazines or blogs, fan cultures, and the countless types of consumer paraphernalia linked to particular programs (t-shirts, soundtracks, books, ring tones, etc.) are vital in understanding how television texts function as sites of cultural production and consumption.

This article puts forth a new methodology for studying lesbians on television and in other image-based popular cultural texts that focuses on questions of production and consumption rather than representation. While Chambers focuses on how queer television texts produce normative meanings around sex, gender, and sexuality, our discussion moves beyond this to ask how these sex/gender norms are produced and governed alongside discourses of sexual citizenship, cosmopolitanism and consumption. Keeping *The L Word* as the central case study, we argue that lesbian sexuality and lesbian politics in this program are first and foremost constructed through their investments in certain neoliberal consumer and lifestyle practices that limit the possibility of what lesbian subjectivities and/or lesbian politics can or cannot *do*. While the program periodically offers viewers explicit and risqué "lesbian" sexual encounters and/or provides pseudo-political commentaries on issues such as gays and lesbians in the military, same-sex parenting, interracial relationships, homophobia/transphobia in the workplace, this subject matter is always mediated within a storyline and setting that idealize and normalize elite and exclusive consumptive practices. We offer an alternative strategy for reading lesbians in image-based media and popular culture that attends to the ways in which lesbian subjectivities (along with meanings around class and race) are produced within neoliberal consumer and lifestyle contexts that establish the limits of who the sexual citizen is and the possibilities of what or who they can *become*. Although our analysis focuses primarily on *The L Word*, a drama serial produced in the United States for cable television, our aim is to provide a set of methodological tools that can be applied to other lesbian-themed television texts and to a range of other image-based visual media including film, commercial advertising, and new media.

TELEVISING THE SEXUAL CITIZEN AS COSMOPOLITAN CONSUMER-CITIZEN

Not unlike the concept of citizenship, definitions of sexual citizenship continue to be contested, revised, and reconceived. More recently, scholars of sexual citizenship have focused on the representation of the queer sexual citizen as the ultimate cosmopolitan consumer who is positioned to forgo basic citizenship rights such as equal protection under the law, access to welfare, and equal rights within same-sex relationships, including the right to marriage (Bell and Binnie, 2000; Berlant, 1997; Cossman, 2007; Evans, 1993; Warner, 1999, 2002). At a very simplistic level, being "cosmopolitan" means being open and able to interact with a variety of different "world cultures" (Hannerz, 1990); it describes a group of people who have "become seemingly more diverse, more international, more *worldly*" (Latham, 2006: 92). For the purposes of this discussion however, cosmopolitanism also encompasses a political economy from within which an entire set of cultural and consumer practices define and govern what it means to be a cosmopolite (Beck, 2004; Latham, 2006). In other words, in this article cosmopolitanism not only identifies and describes the qualities or characteristics of the cosmopolitan citizen, it also considers the discursive and material (although these are by no means independent of one another) processes, practices, and technologies with which one comes to name or describe oneself as cosmopolitan.

In the past three decades being "queer" has become synonymous with being a cosmopolite. The discourse surrounding the pink economy has framed gays and lesbians as an homogenous niche of consumers with a particularly high level of disposable income and leisure time. Their assumed social and spending priorities have located them as part of a particular urban "creative class" whose sensibilities or "tastes" are seen as exemplarily diverse and inclusive (Binnie et al., 2006; Halberstam, 2005). These aesthetic and cultural tastes are not only used to validate queer subjects as respectable sexual citizens, they are also highly consumable attributes. For some straight urban yuppies, participating in and being accepting of queer "difference" function as markers of their own cosmopolitan edge.

The queer sexual citizen as ultimate cosmopolitan consumer has been used to represent gay men on television in series such as Bravo's *Queer Eye for the Straight Guy*, an American reality program premised on the stereotype that gay men have superior taste in fashion, cuisine, interior design, culture, and everyday living.[2] The make-over team of gay men became known in the media as the "fab-five," transforming (at least temporarily) the outward appearance, skills, and taste of heterosexual men making them more desirable for female partners, family, and work colleagues.[3] Brenda Cossman (2007) points out that the "fab-five" occupy a citizenship that "is sexualised beyond heterosexuality, commodified through a celebration of market consumption, and domesticated through a new emphasis on the intimate sphere not only as a site for caring for others but for care of the self" (p. 2). *Queer Eye* strategically positions the gay male make-over team to share homosocial relations with heterosexual men in an effort to improve the latter's personal and professional relations and lifestyle. The "fab-five" engender the new technologies through which citizenship is "being sexed, privatised and self-disciplined" (Cossman, 2007: 2). They function as model neoliberal queer cosmopolitan citizens teaching others how to consume tastefully and how to appropriately work on the self. It is no surprise that the "fab-five" were successful with open mainstream audiences not just for their camp entertainment value, but also because they were instrumental in securing heteronormative romantic, personal, and professional relations for straight men and again, functioned as an onscreen entrée into a certain type of cosmopolitan living. Viewers at home can enjoy the antics of the "fab five," and even empathize with the straight make-overee's need for a queer cosmopolitan intervention.

In their introduction to the edited collection, *Cosmopolitan Urbanism*, Jon Binnie, Julian Holloway, Steve Millington, and Craig Young argue that being a cosmopolitan citizen is a "classed phenomenon" (Binnie et al., 2006: 8) linked to various tenets of cultural citizenship:

> [Cosmopolitanism] is bound up with notions of knowledge, cultural capital and education: being worldly, being able to navigate between and within different cultures, requires confidence, skill and money. . . . [A] cosmopolitan disposition is most often associated with transnational elites that have risen to power and visibility in the neo-liberal era. (pp. 8–9)

In making this link between cosmopolitanism and class, Binnie et al. argue that to be a cosmopolitan subject is to have and/or to have access to certain bodies of knowledge, particular sociocultural norms, particular experiences of urban living, specific types of consumption, a certain level of education, and so on. The *Queer Eye* make-overees are invited to view themselves as subjects in the making, striving to be part of an urban cultural elite that is just beyond their (geographic, sociocultural, and economic) reach. Being part of this grouping is made possible by the queer lifestyle sensibilities and cultural and consumptive "know how" of the Fab Five.

Perhaps unsurprisingly, given the historical position of the lesbian in mainstream culture, there has never been a *Queer Eye for the Straight Woman*—a reality program in which a team of lesbians offer heterosexual women lifestyle and other sociocultural tips.[4] Given the demise of ABC network's *Ellen*—a television sitcom that followed the life, friends, and family of bookstore owner Ellen Morgan (Ellen DeGeneres)—just under a year after the protagonist "came out" in Season Five of the show, the success of *The L Word* is notable.[5] In this context, we constitute success by *The L Word's* four-year run and its multiple nominations for both Emmy and GLAAD media awards. There have been other television programs featuring queer female characters, including *Roseanne, Friends, Queer As Folk, ER, Bad Girls*, and *The Wire*, but openly queer female protagonists have not taken the lead in any other television series.[6] In her critique of *Ellen*, Anna McCarthy (2001) comments that the "fear of a quotidian, ongoing lesbian life on television suggests that, although the network could support queer television as a spectacular media event, it could not sanction a lesbian invasion of serial television's more modest form of history making, the regularly scheduled weeks of televisual flow" (p. 597). Throughout the later stages of the broadcast of *Ellen*, queer television could only act as an interruption to largely heteronormative programming, but televising lesbianism as everyday life not only constituted "adult content" for a formerly prime time sitcom, but also threatened the heteronormative conventions of the sitcom genre. As viewers might remember, Ellen Morgan's coming out narrative "on screen" was paralleled by a media frenzy around Degeneres' own coming out as a lesbian on the cover of *Time* magazine, and in an interview with daytime talk-show host, Oprah Winfrey. In subsequent episodes the program focused on Morgan's efforts to find comic relief in the face of her personal interactions with straight friends and family members.

Premiering six years later, *The L Word* stages precisely the difficulties McCarthy (2001) identified in the ongoing broadcast of *Ellen*, "that same-sex desire plays a deeply agonistic role in the unfolding of temporal structures associated with television's modes of (auto)historiography—the media event, the television schedule, the season run, the final episode" (p. 597). *The L Word* creates a lesbian televisual world where an audience is invited to consume lesbian "diversity" within a carefully orchestrated cosmopolitan setting. Whereas Degeneres functioned as a queer interruption to an otherwise heteronormative television schedule, the conventionally beautiful cast of *The L Word* are consumed in a highly stylized lesbian world that normalizes same-sex desire by mediating it against a range of heteronormative lifestyle consumer choices.

Many of the characters in the series are successful subjects of neoliberalism (and the decline of the Keynesian welfare state) and model cosmopolitan consumers who ably negotiate their economic well-being regardless of personal circumstances. By ensuring their future through the market, individuals are encouraged to live "as if making a project of themselves" (Rose, 1996: 157). Not unlike *Queer Eye*, *The L Word* mediates the character narratives of the lesbian protagonists alongside discourses of urban cosmopolitan living and self-transformation. Helena Peabody (Rachel Shelley), director of her family's foundation, is an independently wealthy heiress representing the queer sexual citizen as ultimate consumer until her mother cuts her off from the family fortune in an effort to teach Helena not just to curb her spendthrift habits, but also that money cannot buy you love. In Season Four, the audience gets to know a penniless and desperate Helena who gets involved in a suspect relationship with a wealthy woman named Catherine because, as she admits, she is simply "not cut out to live modestly." Keeping with the conventions of serial drama, in Season Five, Helena ends up stealing from Catherine. After a stint in prison where Helena falls in love with her "butch" cell-mate, she leaves the pressures of LA life behind to live on a beach with her new lover (who we find out is not a seasoned criminal either but an ex-accountant who embezzled money). Having learned the value of money "the hard way," Helena is gifted with her family fortune once again and returns to her Hollywood Hill's life, Paris Hilton style. Although Helena does curb her once excessive levels of consumption and chooses to live a little more modestly after her stint in prison, her new lifestyle is still marked by many of the privileges associated with cosmopolitan consumer practices. Similarly, Bette Porter (Jennifer Beals), art curator and Dean of the California University School of Arts, engenders a very particular type of cultural citizenship; her former relationship with Tina (Laurel Holloman) reflects upper-middle-class values visible through her lifestyle—she has a palatial home, expensive works of art, a large swimming pool, and other luxury personal and household items. The first season of the series focuses on Bette and Tina conceiving a child using donor insemination, and when the two key characters' relationship eventually breaks down both women are able to maintain financially comfortable lifestyles. Even the formerly homeless Shane McCutcheon (Katherine Moennig)—hairdresser for the inner-urban chic set—is the ultimate sexual consumer (rumored to have slept with over 960 women according to the series' website, http://www.sho.com/site/lword) whose financial status wavers from a baseline of self-sufficiency, depending on whether she is dating a woman who has money to boost her lifestyle, however temporarily.[7] While various characters lose (Helena Peabody) or accrue wealth (Jennifer Schecter), the audience is privy not only to didactic lessons of character and integrity, but also witness to the technologies of self-governance, self-mastery, and self-transformation lesbian and queer citizens are encouraged to embody in order to constitute themselves as successful consumer-citizens. Sexual citizens who fail to adequately self-manage risk their comfort and security within the domains of family, market, and sexual relations.

COSMOPOLITAN GIRLS DOING NEOLIBERAL POLITICS

As the quotation by Sedgwick used in the introduction of this article illustrates, after the first season of *The L Word* premiered, critics commented on the program's inadequate engagement with political debates relevant to the everyday lives of "real" lesbians (Wolfe & Roripaugh, 2006) and on its lack of concern for the complex ways in which class and race are signified within queer "communities" (Sedgwick, 2004). Ilene Chaiken's candid response that everyone would eventually find themselves in the succeeding seasons' cast line-ups suggests that writers and producers attempted to "diversify" the scope of lesbian representations on offer in the show. In Season Two, the series' writers introduce Carmen de la Pica Morales (Sarah Shahi), the Latina DJ from East LA. Season Three explores the transphobia experienced both within and outside the lesbian community by introducing Moira/Max Sweeny (Daniela Sea), a female-to-male transgender character from America's Midwest.[8] Season Three features Dana Fairbanks' (Erin Daniels) fight against breast cancer and in Seasons Four and Five the silencing and surveillance of gays and lesbians in the military is developed by introducing the African- American character Tasha Williams (Rose Rollins). As we stated before, it is not the aim of our analysis to argue whether or not introducing more "racially or sexually diverse" character storylines does or does not allow the series to more accurately reflect "true" lesbian diversity, nor is our focus on asking whether or not the addition of certain storylines renders *The L Word* more or less politically salient. The shift in methodology suggested here situates these additions of "diversity and difference" within a broader set of questions about how neoliberal governmental order defines and normalizes sexual citizens first and foremost through discourses of cosmopolitan consumerism. In other words, our focus is on asking how the politics of sex/gender identity and the intersections between issues of race, class, gender, and sexuality are produced from within increasingly normalized models of cosmopolitan consumer citizenship and how these models function smoothly and easily within the context of mainstream/cable television. We want to understand how *The L Word's* portrayal of certain sociopolitical or cultural issues is mediated within a neoliberal framework and within a rationalized television soap-opera genre that defines sexual citizens through discourses of consumption (of objects, of self, and of others) and self-transformation. The examples offered in this article provide a starting point for this task, asking not what the *The L Word is*, but rather what it *does*.

In Season Four two new characters are introduced, Papi Torres (Janina Gavankar), *The L Word's* Latina Casanova, and Tasha Williams (Rose Rollins), a captain in the United States National Guard who is temporarily on leave from a tour in Iraq. Both of these characters offer the cast of core characters who are predominately White and unashamedly middle class the ultimate cosmopolitan experience—an opportunity to imagine lesbian life outside the confines of The Planet (Kit Porter's "lesbian friendly" local café and night spot where the core cast of characters frequently meet) and beyond the chic, trendy façade of West Hollywood. Papi is first introduced as a sexually and socially mysterious character. When Papi's number of registered "hook ups" crashes Alice's online social network, "The Chart," Alice is determined to meet the unknown lesbian behind the large number of one night stands who has somehow insinuated herself into Alice's elite social circle. After scouring the "foreign" clubs and streets of East LA, Alice finally meets Papi (who is working as a limousine driver), experiences a night of sexual bliss, and uncharacteristically accepts the limitations of her casual encounter, explaining to her friends: "that's just Papi." In succeeding episodes, Papi is almost seamlessly integrated into the show's key storylines and into the daily comings and goings of lesbian life at The Planet, even though Papi remains dismissive of the middle-class privileged and largely White (except Bette Porter portrayed by Jennifer Beals and Kit Porter portrayed by Pam Grier) cultural backgrounds of her new acquaintances.[9] Unlike Tasha, Papi's character is allowed little development other than a hyperbolic performance of sexual consumption that challenges Shane's (Katherine Moennig) similar reputation. *The L Word* writers frame the first meeting between Papi and Shane as a pastiche of a standoff from Sergio Leone's 1966 Italian epic spaghetti western, *The Good, The Bad and the Ugly*.[10] While Shane remains indifferent to Papi's appearance on her "turf," Papi's antagonism and competitiveness with Shane is framed in terms of racial difference—she wants to be a more successful sexual consumer than the "little White girl" she calls "vanilla spice" who appears to consume women so effortlessly. While Papi's sexual consumption exceeds Shane's, Papi is required to put much more effort and self-work into her sexual and gendered performance than Shane, who instead, seems to stumble into her sexual encounters.

Although both Papi (Latina) and Tasha (African American) increase the "diversity" of lesbian representation, both characters continue to occupy outsider status because they operate as the only suburban, working-class lesbian "Others" amid a cast of middle- and upper-middle-class characters. Ulrich Beck (2004) maintains that cosmopolitan citizenship feeds an economy of excess that depends on the fetishization and consumption of the Other. He writes:

> Cosmopolitanism has itself become a commodity; the glitter of cultural difference fetches a good price. Images of an in-between world, of the black body, exotic beauty, exotic music, exotic food and so on, are globally cannibalised, re-staged and consumed as produces for mass markets. (pp. 150–151)

For Beck, the desire to be more cosmopolitan, to acquire the quality of "being worldly" is about making a number of consumer choices—travelling to certain "exotic" places, watching certain anthropological television documentaries, eating in certain "ethnic" suburbs—that overlook the operations of power and give majoritarian cultures cause and permission to consume minoritarian Others. As we have emphasized throughout this article, *The L Word* positions its key lesbian characters as cosmopolitan consumers in a climate of neoliberalism in which consumption is seen to represent the liberties that come with both heteronormative and homonormative citizenship in the United States and in the West more generally. Access to ethnic and racial difference within this televisual lesbian world is thus always bound to consumer and lifestyle practices that fetishize the raced lesbian "Other" and render the White (lesbian) body as the normative or model cosmopolitan sexual citizen.

Both Papi and Tasha also perform their gender differently; while Papi is aggressively charming with women until they sleep with her, Tasha's understated, reserved performance of female masculinity (Halberstam, 1998; Davies, 2007, 2008a) situates her, at least within the parameters of *The L Word*, as "the butch." In addition to Rollins' performance of masculinity, Alice—who takes a sexual interest in Tasha—comments that Tasha seems "angry." If, as Judith Halberstam (1998) notes, "blackness in general is associated with excessive and indeed violent masculinity in the social imaginary" (p. 29), then Rollins exploits this by retaining what might be perceived as traditionally working-class values (the unquestioning commitment to fight the war in Iraq to *protect* her country) and her remarkably polite middle-class performance of masculinity in scenes of courtship with Alice. However, *The L Word's* casting choice of Rose Rollins as a butch character is not uncomplicated given her successful career as a model in New York.[11] Because "masculinity and femininity signify as normative within and through white middle-class heterosexual bodies" (Halberstam, 1998: 29), as Halberstam notes, Tasha's performance of masculinity on *The L Word* sits alongside off-screen interviews in which she identifies herself as heterosexual and alludes to her successful modelling career.[12] As Evans (1993) argues, "the progressive sexualisation of modern capitalist societies is primarily shaped by the complex interrelated material interests of the market and state" (p. i). While Rollins' presence is critical in relation to Black butch representation to "undo hierarchized relations between dominant and minority masculinities" (Halberstam, 1998: 29), the extra-textual dimension of the choice to cast a former model is shaped by perceived material interests of the televisual consumer market. Once again we have an incident where lesbianism functions as a momentary interruption, but does not entirely destablize the conventions of the genre or the desires of straight viewers.

Tasha's position as captain in the U.S National Guard does, however, raise significant issues about the role of lesbians in the military and the infamous "Don't ask, Don't tell" campaign introduced as a compromise measure and signed off by President Bill Clinton.[13] The policy, crafted by Colin Powell, went against Clinton's campaigning for presidency in which he had promised all citizens the right, regardless of sexual orientation, to serve openly in the military—a departure from the complete ban on gays serving in the military. Elsewhere Davies (2008b) argues that the fiction of heterosexuality is still compulsory within the Uniform Code of Military Justice in which sodomy is illegal for members of the U.S. armed forces—a group of citizens whose role is explicitly understood to both represent and embody the nation and thus, heteronormativity. In the context of *The L Word*, Tasha's patriotism for her country clashes with Alice's disapproval of America's involvement in the invasion of and war in Iraq. Unable to give up her relationship with Alice, and after being spotted publicly by others in the military including a fellow comrade who wants Tasha's job, Tasha is investigated for homosexual misconduct. Two homophobic military officers visit Alice at her home, questioning her about the nature of her relations with Tasha and create an uncomfortable scene in which Alice surreptitiously hides a picture of her with Tasha.

This scene contrasts with Captain Beech's visit to Alice's apartment in the succeeding episode. A senior colleague of Tasha's who is also the legal representative in the case mounted against her, Captain Beech, is initially highly antagonistic around Tasha's efforts to defend herself. In a gesture of support and reconciliation, Captain Beech arrives at Alice's apartment with his wife who has clearly convinced him to rethink his position. Alice's femininity and supposedly wife-like qualities are compared to his own wife's, while Captain Beech positions Tasha's performance of masculinity alongside his own. In this instance, Alice and Tasha's gender performances are read through a discourse of heteronormativity likening the butch-femme dynamic to that produced in conventional heterosexual relations, and thus mediating the women's lesbian relationship. The attractiveness of the lesbian couple also contributes to Captain Beech's shift in opinion from being negative, to his being convinced to support Tasha's case. In this context, the gaze of the White authoritative heterosexual male authenticates lesbian existence. The conventional attractiveness of the women, their harmonious management of their class and racial differences, and the recontextualization of their performances of gender within a conventional heteronormative framework, allows Captain Beech to produce an account of Tasha as an adequately patriotic citizen. As Cossman (2007) notes, normalization is a strategy for inclusion in the prevailing social norms and institutions of family, gender, work, and nation. This strategy neutralizes the significance of sexual difference (and in the case of this example, of racial difference) and sexual identity, particularly of those subjects who, in every other way, reproduce ideal citizenship (Cossman, 2007; Seidman, 1997). This example of the U.S military's stance on sexual minorities shows that the state plays a powerful role not only in pathologizing identities, but also in producing them.[14]

We argue that *The L Word* and other television programming with queer content, shapes and produces lesbian subjectivity beyond the onscreen fictional world viewers are offered. Tasha and Alice's capacity to pass as "acceptably" heteronormative negates the discriminatory measures taken against lesbians and gays in the U.S. military by the nation-state "off screen." While the *The L Word* draws attention to the discriminatory measures of the American government, the critique of this discrimination is mediated alongside the ideals and values of neoliberalism and cosmopolitanism. Tasha and Alice pass as acceptable queer citizens because their performances of gender become intelligible through a heterosexual cosmopolitan matrix. Beech "comes out" as a lesbian ally by adopting a more cosmopolitan view of difference. Alice and Tasha's difference lends weight to his character development and allows him to remain bound to his core values, heterosexuality, family, and patriotism. However, viewers are left wondering whether Tasha would have gained Captain Beech's support without the feminine, White, and tastefully presented Alice by her side. Situating a critique of this discrimination in the context of neoliberalism and its attendant practices of cosmopolitanism and consumption offers a new set of methodological tools for studying lesbian image-based texts in popular and mediated cultures. Rather than simply critiquing the normative representations *The L Word* offers its viewers, our analysis situates the text's capacity to disrupt normative models of sexual citizenship within a broader sociopolitical context.

CONCLUSION

We began this article by suggesting that questions of representation limit critiques of lesbian image-based texts for they focus solely on what the text *is* or *is not*. Our concern lies with what lesbian image-based texts *do*. We put forth an alternative methodology for reading lesbians on television and in other popular cultural texts that asks how lesbian subjectivities and notions of lesbian "politics" are *produced* and *governed* alongside emerging models of cosmopolitan consumer citizenship. Showtime's *The L Word* offers a useful case study. Throughout this article we have argued that unlike other television shows featuring lesbian content, this program offers viewers a fictional West Hollywood lesbian-centered milieu whose intimate desires are shaped and produced by neoliberal consumer and lifestyle practices. Investing lesbians with limited forms of consumer power, *The L Word* produces sexual citizens who purchase their sexual identities while conceding partial citizenship rights, thus limiting the possibility of what lesbian subjectivities and lesbian politics can become. In developing our analysis we also illustrated how the addition of "racial and ethnic difference" into the program's storyline is used to solidify normative models of cosmopolitan sexual citizenship. Characters from "diverse" cultural backgrounds are used by the program to add depth and interest to plots and storylines about an otherwise very White portrayal of queer living.

NOTES

1. *The L Word* is a television drama series portraying the lives of lesbian, bisexual, and queer women in Los Angeles. Ilene Chaiken is the executive producer and creator, along with Steve Goiln and Larry Kennar. The pilot episode premiered to a North American audience on January 18, 2004, and the fifth season screened on January 6, 2008.

2. *Queer Eye for the Straight Guy* premiered on the Bravo cable television network on July 15, 2003. The series was created by David Collins and David Metzler, and produced by their production company, Scout Productions.

3. The team includes: Ted Allen, Kyan Douglas, Thom Filicia, Carson Kressley, and Jai Rodriguez.

4. As Lynda Hart (1994) has commented, lesbians in mainstream representation have almost always been depicted as predatory, dangerous, and pathological.

5. The ABC network's *Ellen* premiered on American television on March 29, 1994, finishing on July 22, 1998, running for 109 episodes.

6. Produced by Showtime and Cable Street Productions, *Queer as Folk* is an American and Canadian co-production based on the British series with the same title. The series ran for five seasons between 2000–2005 on Showtime and 2001–2005 on Showcase.

7. "Shane is rumored to have slept with a little over 960 women in her lifetime, dating back to the tender age of just 14 years old." Showtime's Official *The L Word* website, accessed 8th March 8, 2008, http://lwordwiki.sho.com/page/Shane+McCutcheon?t = anon

8. Jenny meets Moira/Max in Skokie, Illinois when she returns home for medical care. Moira/Max is originally from Wilmett, Illinois.

9. In *The L Word* both Latina characters are played by non-Latina actors. Sarah Shahi (Carmen) has an Iranian father and Spanish mother and grew up in Dallas, Texas. Janina Gavanka (Papi) is from a Dutch-Indian family and grew up in Illinois. These casting decisions suggest that the "Otherness" of the "non-White" characters in the show is somehow universal and that the specificities of their ethnic differences are insignificant to the storyline and will not register with viewers.

10. *The Good, the Bad and the Ugly*. Dir. Sergio Leone, United Artists, 1966.

11. *The L Word* Online, http://www.thelwordonline.com/tasha.html (accessed March 10), 2008.

12. Shauna Swartz, "Interview With *The L Word*'s Rose Rollins," http://www.logoonline.com/news/story.jhtml?id=1552891&disableFeatureRedirect=true&contentTypeID=1300 (accessed March 10, 2008).

13. The "Don't ask, don't tell" policy is officially known as Pub.L. 103–160 (10 U.S.C. § 654). Unless one of the exceptions from 10 U.S.C. § 654(b) applies, the policy prohibits anyone who "demonstrate(s) a propensity or intent to engage in homosexual acts" from serving in the United States armed forces because apparently it "would create an unacceptable risk to the high standards of morale, good order and discipline, and unit cohesion that are the essence of military capability."

14. See Cristyn Davies, "Proliferating panic: regulating representations of sex and gender during the culture wars," *Cultural Studies Review*, 14(2), 2008: 83–102.

REFERENCES

Akass, K. and J. McCabe, eds. *Reading The L Word: Outing Contemporary Television*. London: I.B. Tauris, 2006.

Beck, U. "Cosmopolitan Realism: On the Distinction Between Cosmopolitanism in Philosophy and the Social Sciences," *Global Networks*, 4, 2004: 131–156

Becker, R. *Gay TV and Straight America*. New Brunswick, NJ: Rutgers University Press, 2004.

Beirne, R. "Fashioning The L Word," *Nebula*, 3(4), 2006. http://www.nobleworld.biz/; Accessed March 10, 2008.

_____. "Dirty Lesbian Pictures: Art and Pornography in *The L Word*," *Critical Studies in Television*, 2(1), 2007: 90–101.

Bell, D. and J. Binnie. *The Sexual Citizen: Queer Politics and Beyond*. Cambridge: Polity Press, 2000.

Benshoff, H. and S. Griffin. *Queer Images: A History of Gay and Lesbian Film in America*. New York: Rowman & Littlefield Publishers Inc, 2006.

Berlant, L. *The Queen of America Goes to Washington City: Essays on Sex and Citizenship*. Durham, NC: Duke University Press, 1997.

Binnie, J., J. Holloway, S. Millington, and C. Young, eds. *Cosmopolitan Urbanism*. London: Routledge, 2006.

Chambers, S. (2006). "Heteronormativity and *The L Word*: From a Politics of Representation to a Politics of Norms." In K. Akass and J. McCabe, eds. *Reading The L Word: Outing Contemporary Television*. London: I.B. Tauris, 2006: 81–98.

Chasin, A. *Selling Out: The Gay and Lesbian Movement Goes to Market*. New York: St. Martin's Press., 2000

Cossman, B. *Sexual Citizens: The Legal and Cultural Regulation of Sex and Belonging*. Stanford, CA: Stanford University Press, 2007.

Davies, C. "Disturbing the Dialectics of the Public Toilet," *Hecate: An Interdisciplinary Journal of Women's Liberation, 33*(2), 2007: 120–134.

———. "Becoming Sissy: A Response to David McInnes." In B. Davies, ed. *Judith Butler in Conversation: Analyzing the Texts and Talk of Everyday Life*. New York: Routledge, 2008a.

———. "Proliferating Panic: Regulating Representations of Sex and Gender During the Culture Wars," *Cultural Studies Review, 4*(2), 2008b: 83–102.

Doty, A. *Making Things Perfectly Queer: Interpreting Mass Culture*. Minneapolis: University of Minnesota Press, 1993.

———. *Flaming Classics: Queering the Film Canon*. New York: Routledge, 2000.

Dow, B. (2008). "Ellen, Television and the Politics of Gay and Lesbian Visibility." In C. Brunsdon and L. Spigel, eds. *Feminist Television Criticism: A Reader*. New York: Open University Press, 2008.

Evans, D. T. *Sexual Citizenship: The Material Construction of Sexualities*. London: Routledge, 1993.

Halberstam, J. *Female Masculinity*. Durham, NC: Duke University Press, 1998.

———. *In a Queer Time and Place: Transgender Bodies, Subcultural Lives*. New York: New York University Press, 2005.

Hannerz, U. (1990). "Cosmopolitans and Locals in World Culture," *Theory, Culture & Society, 7*(2), 1990: 237–251.

Hart, L. *Fatal Women: Lesbian Sexuality and the Mark of Aggression*. Princeton, NJ: Princeton University Press, 1994.

Kabir, S. *Daughters of Desire: Lesbian Representations in Film*. London: Cassell, 1998.

Latham, A. "Sociality and the Cosmopolitan Imagination: National, Cosmopolitan and Local Imaginaries in Auckland, New Zealand." In J. Binnie, J. Holloway, S. Millington, and C. Young, eds. *Cosmopolitan Urbanism*. London: Routledge, 2006: 89–111.

Mayne, J. *Framed: Lesbians, Feminists and Media Culture*. Minneapolis: University of Minnesota Press, 2000.

McCarthy, A. "Ellen: Making Queer Television History", *GLQ: A Journal of Lesbian and Gay Studies*, 7(4), 2001: 593–620.

Patton, C. (1995). "What is a Nice Lesbian Like You Doing in a Film Like This?" In T. Wilton, ed. *Immortal, Invisible: Lesbians and the Moving Image*. London: Routledge, 1995: 20–33.

Rich, R. "The New Queer Cinema." In H. Benshoff and S. Griffin, eds. *Queer Cinema, the Film Reader*. New York: Routledge, 2004: 53–60.

Rose, N. *Inventing Ourselves: Psychology, Power and Personhood*. Cambridge: Cambridge University Press, 1996.

Sedgwick, E. K. "*The L Word*: Novelty and Normalcy," *Chronicle of Higher Education, 50*(19), 2004: B10–B11.

Seidman, S. "From Identity to Queer Politics: Shifts in Normative Heterosexuality." In S. Seidman and J. Alexander, eds. *The New Social Theory Reader*. New York: Routledge, 1997: 353–360.

Sender, K. "Sex Sells: Sex, Class, and Taste in Commercial Gay and Lesbian Media," *GLQ: A Journal of Lesbian and Gay Studies*, 9(3), 2003: 331–365.

———. *Business, Not Politics: The Making of the Gay Market*. New York: Columbia University Press, 2004.

Stacey, J. (1995). "If You Don't Play, You Can't Win: *Desert Hearts* and the Lesbian Romance Film." In T. Wilton, ed. *Immortal, Invisible: Lesbians and the Moving Image*. London: Routledge, 1995: 92–114.

Warner, M. *The Trouble with Normal: Sex, Politics, and the Ethics of Queer Life*. New York: Free Press, 1999.

———. *Publics and Counterpublics*. New York: Zone Books, 2002.

Weiss, A. *Vampires and Violets: Lesbians in the Cinema*. London: Cape, 1992.

Whatling, C. *Screen Dreams: Fantasising Lesbians in Film*. Manchester: Manchester University Press, 1997.

White, P. *Uninvited: Classical Hollywood Cinema and Lesbian Representability*. Bloomington: Indiana University Press, 1999.

Wolfe, S. J. and L. A. Roripaugh. "The (In)visible Lesbian: Anxieties of Representation in *The L Word*." In K. Akass and J. McCabe, eds. *Reading The L Word: Outing Contemporary Television*. London: I.B. Tauris, 2006: 43–54.

Complexities and Complications: Intersections of Class and Sexuality

YVETTE TAYLOR

I explore some questions and dilemmas raised by considering social class, gender, and sexuality within the same interconnecting research framework. I begin with attention to the theoretical development of intersectionality, arising from feminist conceptualizations of "differences that matter," and the ways these are included in or excluded from research agendas. Arguing that interconnections between class and sexuality have often been neglected in such moves, I seek to progress beyond intersectionality as a theoretical paradigm, toward understanding intersectionality as a lived experience. I draw on a case study of working-class lesbian lives to bridge the gap between theorization of intersectionality and the research application of this.

FIRST STEPS: INTRODUCING INTERSECTIONS

This article explores the limitations, exclusions, and possibilities of intersectional analysis. Nearly twenty years after the term *intersectionality* was first coined it remains a vital concept within feminism (Crenshaw, 1993). Yet its significance does not go unquestioned, where its easy 'buzzword' status (Davis, 2008) may serve to sideline continued interrogation of inequalities in the sweep of what we "already know." Here the specific legacies and endurances of the term are somewhat effaced, alongside a disappearance of specific inequalities, which risks a return of the "geometry inspired" hierarchical list of what counts (Weston, 1996). Feminist scholars have assessed the advantages and limitations of intersectionality as a research methodology and a body of theory (McCall, 2005); specifically, intersectionality refers to the mutually constrictive nature of social divisions and the ways these are experienced, reproduced, and resisted in everyday life. A successful intersectional practice thus explores relational and reinforcing exclusions and inclusions, the first steps of which are to identify and name these. In the case of class and sexuality this is indeed both complex and complicated. Drawing on research on self-identified working-class lesbians in the United Kingdom, I demonstrate the ways that class and sexuality are intertwined, as embodied, material and subjective realities: the repeated separation and situation as *either* "material" (class) *or* "queer" (sexuality) constitutes an intersectional absence and erasure.

I seek to be mindful of the legacies of the concept, emerging out of Black feminist critique of the lack of "race" in feminist theorizing. Such contestations have not only taken place in response to mainstream feminism but rather actively inform and constitute its development (Anthias and Yuval-Davis, 1983; Anthias, 2002; Brah and Phoenix, 2004). To ignore this may well be to advance specific claims of ownership of intersectionality and reduce its wider applicability, where "race" is dropped out of intersectional practice, with class (Acker, 2008) and sexuality (Schilt, 2008) even more under-theorized. In contrast, I see intersectional theorization and practice reaching beyond the specific examples that I present in this article; many have commented on the challenges, absences, and necessities of intersectional approaches and I situate my argument and approach among these (Berger and Guidroz, 2009).

The claim that class and sexuality *do* intersect is not new. "Intersection" is now a common trope in discussion of identities and social locations, whereby sexuality becomes another potential spoke on the "intersectional wheel" (Anthias, 2001, 2002; Brah and Phoenix, 2004). That said, in the case of class and sexuality intersections are often gestured toward without being fully unpacked or empirically apparent. Research among lesbian and gay populations has overly relied on and recruited samples from fairly privileged, White, middle-class groups instigating my initial motivating question of "where are the working-class lesbians?" (Taylor, 2005, 2007a).

Debates on "intersections" force an awareness of the social divisions that are thought of as still relevant, as against those that are seen as simply old and settled, variously casting inequalities as embellishments or deletions, the component parts of "class," "gender," "sexuality' to be added or scored out for flavor and fashion (McLaughlin, 2006). In considering intersectionality, it seems urgent to think about what matters and why, given that all junctions are not equally picturesque or dangerous.

Feminist theory and research has long struggled with matters of identity and difference, particularly in terms of gender, sexuality, race, and class. From second wave feminism to supposedly "post-feminist" times, such issues have been cast as prime concerns or ignored realities (Richardson,

McLaughlin, and Casey, 2006). Although feminism has achieved a certain institutional credence and more thorough and complex understandings of women's lives, within this move of (ambivalent) institutional authorization it would be naïve to think that all feminist concerns have entered this space evenly. Often the most excluded are not included or invited into mainstreamed arguments, theories, and actions—yet such groups do not exist solely as the jaggy elbow nudging on "our" feminist agendas, or as the outsiders awaiting an invitation. Echoing McCall's (2005) concerns in discussing "The Complexity of Intersectionality," I too expect more of feminist research and seek to hold it to a higher standard. This article represents an attempt to show and convince, a demand to "get it," while paying heed to the complexity of assertion and silence; the intersections that I chart in my research are also personal passions and pains, unsolved by the rolling of eyes, academic or otherwise.

There are different, even competing, definitions of "intersectionality" and I will explore how class, gender, and sexuality figure in these debates and the consequences this has for which women are included in feminist theory and research. Notions of "intersectionality" have developed from initial attempts at identifying crossover points in axes of difference, such as gender, "race," and class, to more sophisticated attempts at highlighting their mutual construction, embeddedness, and movement, rather than static being. It is important, although difficult, to speak of intersecting categories without becoming grid locked in claims and denials. Another difficulty lies in understanding the everyday experience of this connection and I turn to my empirical data on working-class lesbians' lives in order to illuminate the tension between the theoretical complexities of intersectionality and the research appliance of this, where multiplicity is hard, although not impossible, to navigate.

INTERSECTIONAL RE-RUNS: INCLUSIONS AND EXCLUSIONS

The branches of Materialist (or Socialist/Marxist), Black and Lesbian Feminism, associated with second wave feminisms, are now fractured and contested in "postmodernist," queer times (Richardson et al., 2006). However, the issues that these feminisms articulated continue, demonstrating that such dilemmas are neither new nor solved. Materialist feminism, for example, has foregrounded gender and class structures in explaining women's oppression (Hennessy, 2006; Jackson, 2006), a perspective that has been criticized as universalizing women's oppression. Gender inequality is attributed a primary significance rather than paying heed to the ways in which differently positioned women are advantaged and disadvantaged by classed, gendered, sexual, and racial inequalities, as other central and intersectional social divisions (Mirza, 1997; Berger, 2004; Taylor, 2007a).

Black feminism challenged initial analyses of patriarchy and capitalism, pointing to the ways that arrangements and meanings of "the family" are differentiated for Black women and men, just as the division of labor is also racialized. Sojourner Truth's phrase, "Aint I a Woman?," acting as a powerful question mark echoing across time and place, underscores the complexity of the construction "woman," revealing that the "commonality" of this category was in fact based on the intersectional experiences of the very few (White, middle-class, heterosexual women) (Crenshaw, 1993). Lesbian feminists also asserted their mis/matches within mainstream feminism, where they were often depicted as messing with a singularly respectable feminist cause or as stragglers who would be dealt with when the *real* fight had been won (Jeffreys, 2003). A return to such initial dilemmas serves as a reminder of the historical inclusions and exclusions within feminist theory and research.

The range and shape of feminist concerns shifts across time, being redrawn and contested in a "new" climate of "third wave," even "post-feminist," times (Richardson and Robinson, 2007). Yet the shoring up of feminist "waves" often serves to demarcate a false divide between "then" and "now"; divergent and common paths of feminisms continue to be carved out and the repeated challenge lies in highlighting overlaps, interconnections, and distinctions. For some, new times represent new ways of dealing with intersectionality, bridging the complexity of multiple identity categories and interconnected experiences but there can be scepticism and concern over what is retained and what is lost. I share this uncertainty in terms of the apparent separation between class and sexuality, or between the "material" and the "queer."

Queer theory now sets much of the agenda on sexuality studies, displacing many feminist contributions in this area (Richardson et al., 2006). A significant challenge therefore lies in thinking through the intersection between feminist and queer theory rather than deleting one as naïvely universal and the other as relativistic and politically meaningless. Anzaldúa (1988) suggested that the term "queer" originated in Black and Latina working-class cultures having little to do with respectable academia, constituting another erasure in claims (re)made regarding disciplinary credence; what really counts and who knows best. In playing out these intersectional re-runs the trick is not to be bound by claims, concessions, and negations but rather to find a way through, around, and with identities, experiences, and practices; recent re-visitations of intersectionality have sought to do just that, speaking of "situated positionality" and "hybridity." In charting out such theoretical developments, the fact of "intersectionality" as an experience, rather than a benign listing, or as purely cultural representation, often still needs attention. Plummer summarizes this sentiment, stating that "There are important studies to be done in the empirical world, and an obsession with texts is dangerous indeed. It is time to move beyond the text—and rapidly" (1998: 611)

WHICH INTERSECTIONS, WHAT EFFECTS? THEORETICAL AND ACTUAL ABSENCES

In re-considering intersectionality and contemporary feminist politics Yuval-Davis (2006) poses the above question in a different way, asking which social divisions matter: What is useful, additional, or simply too weighty? The lure of additive equations appears in the detailing of "double" and "triple" oppression models, furthered by Lutz's (2002) fourteen "lines of difference," which extends the three major players of race, class, and gender to include, for example, sexuality, culture, ability, and age. In extending difference to encompass every dimension of social life there is often concern about the *difference* that difference makes; what really counts and when does a difference become an inequality? The debate can range from exhausted addition to fragmentation and back again, stagnating theoretical frameworks and research agendas.

Rather than portraying intersectionality as a list to be constructed and completed, whereby inequalities are rated and ranked, others have pointed instead to ongoing complexity and multiplicity, so that race, gender, and class cannot simply be "tagged onto each other mechanically" (Anthias and Yuval-Davis, 1983: 62). Phrases such as "translocational positionality" and the "situated accomplishments" of identities are spoken of as bridges between the feminist past and the feminist future, an optimistic one that more adequately conceptualizes the intersection between social divisions. In this model the focus and burden on the disadvantaged to "come out," to reveal themselves and make their position on the intersectional axes known, is potentially displaced by also considering how powerful identities are un/inhabited (Valentine, 2007).

However, a focus on complexity and multiplicity risks losing sight of "old" certainties, giving up that which constitutes and explains; categories become confounded and undone by "complexity" and that which was once prioritized, disappears. This is true of class analysis, troubled and erased from the present, sent back to the distant past. Here "new" intersections risk recasting "old," enduring divisions, as over and finished. The move away from fairly ungendered, quantifiable socioeconomic classifications has inspired increased attention toward the cultural, embodied, and social components of social class. But for this to be an intersectional gain the connecting material, subjective, embodied, and spatial dimensions of class and sexuality cannot be separated. And while we are all implicated in class and sexuality these categories have more power, purchase, and even pain for some more than others (Skeggs, 1997; Taylor, 2007a).

The shift away from (and return to) class analysis raises the question about the usefulness of the concept of class and whether class itself needs to be revised, troubled, even queered in research practices. Bradley and Hebson (1999) invoke the concept of "class hybridity" as a strategy for approaching class analysis but is this an attempt to make class more "interesting" (to "priv-ileged" knowledge producers)? The concept of hybridity, if all inclusive, per-haps loses its analytical worth. Anthias (2001) explores "hybridity" as a key term in race debates, capable of rejecting ideas of pre-existing "pure" racial categories. Yet the battleground of essentialized articulation versus diffusion is re-visited in referencing and speaking to specific identities/experiences, as against a focus on their ambiguities, de-constructions, and continual re-constitutions. This dichotomy is nevertheless a rather abstract one, a ruse to be revealed in considering intersectionality as a lived experience, inspiring a move from theory to research practice and empirical analysis.

INTERSECTIONAL METHODOLOGIES: "MAPPING THE MARGINS"

As the theoretical dimensions of intersectionality are debated, pinpointed, and contested, these are also empirically researched and really lived: race, class, gender, and sexuality feature in everyday lives beyond the abstract aca-demic page. The term "intersectionality" was introduced by Crenshaw (1993) in "mapping the margins" of Black women's employment experiences in the United States, noting the ways that identity politics frequently conflated and dismissed differences between *and* within groups. The inadequacy of simple additions is set against a model of structural and political intersectionality, contrasting with attempts to produce a "totalizing theory of identity," where every identity category is finally and completely known and achieved. Cren-shaw vividly teases out what "intersectionality" means empirically, where it shapes the lives of women of color, and politically, where it requires a move beyond identity politics, essentialism, and the "deadly (political) silence" of postmodern questioning. Such questioning, in *only* deconstructing cate-gories, is seen to wrongly distort their continued social and political salience. "Intersection" is not an abstract concept, it is something that lives, breathes, and moves.

Other, more recent, feminist studies have also illustrated the connections between social categories. Berger (2004), for example, charts the experiences of women living with HIV/AIDS in North America who endure and resist stigma, across the intersecting axes of race, gender, class, and HIV status. Berger allows for an understanding of "intersection" as an embodied reality, curtailing certain voices and stories. For example, the dominant political voice in HIV/AIDS activism has focused on White, middle-class gay men, while a strategy of coalition building could foster a *political* intersectionality, capable of speaking to race, gender, class, and sexuality.

Despite the aforementioned accounts, there has been little conversation about how intersectionality is researched in practice, without the project be-coming too unwieldy, with too many "add-ons." Feminist sociologists and ge-ographers have all recently asked what the best methodological approaches are to cast light on connected categories as they are lived out and contested. There are multiple approaches and methods for exploring intersectionality but both Valentine (2007) and McCall (2005) highlight the use of the case study approach, which seeks to take an individual's experience and then extrapolate to the broader social location embodied by an individual. Intersectionality is then illustrated as a politically urgent lived experience where the connections between categories are both transparent and troubled. This is an approach I will now use in discussing the intersection of class, gender, and sexuality, with reference to my data of working-class lesbians' lives as a "case study." The reader may judge if the intersectional efforts are mired in confusion, where intersectionality stalls and breaks down, or if the coming together of different axes of difference and inequality illuminates the mutually constituted lived-in experience of class and sexuality.

WORKING-CLASS LESBIANS: AN INTERSECTIONAL CASE STUDY

My aim here is to put the stories and experiences of the fifty-three women who participated in my research back into discussion about the lived experience of intersectionality. Interviewees came from Scotland (the Highlands, Glasgow, and Edinburgh) and England (Yorkshire and Manchester) and took part in my research through a combination of one-to-one, paired, and group interviews (Taylor, 2005). They ranged in age from 16 to 64 years, allowing for diversity and continuation of classed experiences across the life course to be revealed. Yet because working-class lesbians are a "hard to reach" group, it is inevitable that the women I interviewed are not representative of all who may fit this categorization. A significant absence in my own study is the way that ethnicity also structures the participants' classed experiences, although such an absence is not only in terms of the research cohort but rather in the place of ethnicity in the study as a whole. This is intended as acknowledgment of the ways that Whiteness, for the majority of respondents, is a valued form of ethnicity, where Whiteness can also be seen to be lived differently through the modalities of class (Anzaldúa, 1988; Nayak, 2003).

I write from the position of having found my research sample, thus perhaps solving the dilemma of access. Valentine (1995) claims that lesbian spaces exist "if you know what you're looking for" suggesting a link between researchers' identity and possible research access; I believe that my own identifications enabled me to understand where working-class lesbian may be, or rather, that I would have to look beyond commercialized lesbian and gay venues, typically known as "scene spaces." My identifications as a working-class lesbian were consequential in providing an "insider" status, yet because working-class lesbians are not a homogeneous group, neatly gathered and awaiting empirical investigation, issues of sameness *and* difference had to be negotiated. Insider and outsider status impacted on finding interviewees and establishing rapport and elsewhere I have discussed these particular "intersections" elsewhere (Taylor, 2005; Taylor, 2009). Personalized disjunctures and mis-fittings in inhabiting insider/outsider positions can act as realizations of the long-standing feminist declaration of the "personal as political" but full realization of intersectionality requires a move beyond individual researchers' reflexivity, and a move toward empirical exploration.

I found my respondents, their views, and experiences in all the usual sociological enclaves from school settings, families, and work experiences to sexual, leisure, and shopping experiences and it was in these places I sought to put together that which is usually missed out. The repeated "obviousness" of class in interviewees' lives was not taken as straightforward factual accounts—but I tend toward treating such testimonies as theorized and explained "realities" and claims on how class works, rather than assuming that respondents had the experience—and I had the theory. I found class identifications to be ever present and powerful, supported by the persistent echoes of past generations as well as by assured senses of working-class "reality."

Many women spoke of the ways that they "just knew" themselves to be working class; it was both obvious yet, at times, difficult to articulate because of the ways it often operates at a "subconscious," visceral, emotional level (Skeggs, 1997). The emotional and emotive meanings of class challenge the reduction of analysis to mere categories and descriptors, which miss out on any sense of combined negative and positive feelings about being working class. "Contradictory" emotions are expressed about *both* sexual and class identity, as positive choices and positions, yet that are also grounds for discrimination and silence. Michelle (37, Edinburgh) speaks of her sustained and confrontational sense of identity where "For years and years and years I was adamantly working-class, really fucking 'I'm working-class, that's what I am,'" as settling down more comfortably into something she "just is." Many interviewees spoke of the interrelated material and emotional aspects of class positioning, re-telling the complexity of self-positioning alongside material markers and everyday judgments:

> I suppose it's more about a state of mind rather than anything else. I couldn't define why I would class myself as working-class other than I was brought up in a Council house scheme. I didn't necessarily know what working-class was but I knew that's how people saw us, do you know what I mean. (Grace, 30, Edinburgh)
> I think it's about poverty, I think it's about negotiating your way through the education system when people are speaking ways you don't understand em, it's about the kinds of values you grow up with as well ... (Sukhjit, 29, Manchester)

These negotiations could not be easily deflected and were often welcomed and retained, rather than "given up." Faye speaks of the endurance of "historical roots," echoed in Lynn's sense of permanence:

> A lot of people assess class as what you're earning, whether you're working, that's the traditional way of describing it, whether you're below a certain income. But I think I also include historical roots and experiences, where you come from. (Faye, 45, Manchester)
> I mean I think it's something that you can carry with you for the rest of your life 'cause your views and values are all around growing up being working-class so it didn't make any difference when I was earning a lot of money 'cause I am working-class and that's all I'll ever be. (Lynn, 44, Glasgow)

Class was often spoken of as an entrenched social and personal experience, not that which they wanted to, or in fact could, "give up"; it had made its mark and resurfaced in everyday experiences and emotions, entrenched in the attitudes and identifications of interviewees. Although enduring, class was not something that was fixed and finalized in their accounts; rather, it varied with every recollection and every re-occurrence, making a striking impact on continued identifications. Classed terms and judgments continue to circulate and were highly relevant to the women I interviewed in describing their past and ongoing experiences, in saying what and who they are and what they are not, indicating the difficulty and ease in "coming-out," not only in relation to sexuality.

Working-class lesbians spoke about growing up and belonging to certain families and communities, with a sense of pride in their locations. Yet this was often matched by understandings that who they were, and where they lived, were not valued. Moreover, these locations were often the most immediate places where daily inequalities, projected onto imagined futures, were experienced (Taylor, 2004), as Cathy and Becky demonstrate:

> Em, realising at a very young age how restricted my choices were because of that, what you're going to do with your life and what your choices are going to be according to where you're from, the minute you say you're from Maple Grove. (Cathy, 37, Manchester)
> ... it's one of the most deprived areas of Glasgow which is kinda reflected in the facilities and amenities that are in the area like no kinda big sports centres, the shopping centre's very run down, it's very kinda low cost shops ... because you've got postcode G15 you're not going to get a job, you're looking at postcode discrimination so what's the point in trying? (Becky, 22, Edinburgh)

The sense of being "stuck" in place often worked in subjective, spatial, and material tension with desires to find more comfortable locations. Here Jill recounted the "writing on the wall" as a sign that she should move on:

> . . . I suppose the defining moment for me was when I went to go down the village . . . and all the way down on every single wall and every single thing I could see was 'Jill Walker is gay' (laughs). I was just like 'Fuck! This is where I fucking live!', you know. My mum's got really bad eye sight so luckily she never read any of these things. But the thing was it was all the way down the path that my mum walked down to the pub . . . then a couple of months later I was walking through the woods, like the middle of the woods and came to the wee bridge and all over the fucking bridge was the same, I was like 'I really need to go.' (Jill, 29, Edinburgh)

The move away from home space into commercialized scene space in initial "coming outs" was often experienced as far from comfortable or seamless; instead continued classed struggles affected access and belonging in "lesbian spaces" (Taylor, 2007b). Such a tension moves away from the sole focus on scene space as *the* site for examining sexuality: this does not make sense when charting the experiences of working-class lesbians who often cannot comfortably occupy (classed) scene space. Ultimately there was a sense that commercialized scene space was not really *their* space. Fiona speaks of scene space as not being a "free space" referring to the material and emotional costs in such terrain:

> . . . that's the overall feeling that I've had and have about the gay scene which is very commercialised, it's not really a free space to experiment. . . . But it's a predominantly commercially orientated scene, it's orientated around outlets to make money. . . (Fiona, 29, Edinburgh)

Alice speaks of the difficulty in "fitting in," or even more basically, just "getting in," given such classed dynamics:

> . . . I think there is a lack of working-class places and that's a problem for working-class people. So you, em, either assimilate middle-class values, go into expensive places where you don't feel comfortable. So the options are you either stay in a working-class environment where you get you're head kicked in or behave in a more covert manner in a middle-class sphere and be quite happy to accept it. (Alice, 25, Edinburgh)

Such places are not only venues where drinks are bought and music listened to; rather, they are places where sexuality can be affirmed or denied, and Lynn tells of the more emotional struggles and subtleties in accessing scene space, compared with Alice's more physically dangerous predicament:

> Don't like going in there it's like 'Oh I hope nobody sees me!' it's almost like I am a *lesbian*. ... I would've went in there when I was married, I would've had no problem sitting there with pals who were gay but it's different when it's personal, when it becomes you. (Lynn, 44, Glasgow)

Many interviewees never had access to effective support mechanisms to facilitate "outness," or to meet other women, and instead had to meet in potentially "unsafe" places. Processes of "coming-out" may be classed, not only in terms of access to scene spaces but also as a process that "classes" what can and cannot be said to whom. Even home spaces may not be all that comfortable; "coming-out" to friends and families can at times fracture belonging and although this is not unique to working-class families and individuals, there can be classed effects, "opportunities" and limitations on this. Although Sonia notes that her girlfriend's (Joan) family are more open and talkative about their emotions, she demonstrates that openness and expressiveness are not conflict free. Inequalities are still produced here in terms of what can be disclosed and who gets to say what. Sonia is "out" but her family are not out about it, while Joan's "touchy, feely" family do not want to discuss this issue:

> Now, my family's never had a problem with Joan, which is weird, but her family, which is why we don't talk about emotions or whatever, hers are a very huggy, feely—oh God, it was hell. Absolute hell ... my family who don't talk about our feelings and we never discuss it, but yet Joan's never had a problem with my family, you know. But yet touchy feely middle-class family had a big problem with it and it took them ages to acknowledge our relationship. (Sonia, 32, Yorkshire)

Lesbian "sameness" is often positioned at the vanguard of social change, establishing a "transformation" in intimacy (Dunne, 1997; Giddens, 1992), with such accounts frequently glossing over enduring structural inequalities and the ways these are lived out interpersonally. Even those who have been cautious or critical of supposed transformations rarely explore class as a continued factor informing, constraining, and even enhancing intimate relationships.

Further, in relation to transformations in the workplace and their intersections with the domestic sphere, my findings vastly differ from those of Dunne (1997), who suggests that a lesbian lifestyle necessitates and facilitates access to higher female earnings. I think a classing of the differences between these accounts vividly points to the constraints facing working-class lesbians (and indeed to the opportunities available to more privileged lesbians). My respondents were frequently evaluated through classed locations, as where they came from often stood for and indicated what they could be—a judgment enforced in school, both in the playground and more formally in the classroom. The heterosexualized schooling environment and curriculum have been highlighted by many (Epstein, 1994; Mac an Ghaill, 1996; Skeggs, 1997) but the interaction of "coming-out" about both a stigmatized sexual identity as well as a "deviant" class position, is a rather different and disturbing one, and many simply "slipped out of the system." Having already been deemed "failures" in school many women left with few qualifications and entered low-paid jobs, Youth Training Schemes, or voluntary work placements. Far from being an "economic achievement" (Dunne, 1997), being a lesbian can be a factor leading to disadvantage—combined with class, the "achievement" would seem to diminish. Thus, there are many areas and issues that interconnect the material, embodied, structural, and spatial aspects of class and sexuality, situating lives lived through, on, and in-between these terms. This is primarily highlighted by the empirical data presented, situated within feminist research practices and theorizations form these.

I have considered some questions and dilemmas raised in exploring class, gender, and sexuality within the same research framework, elaborating on the experiential aspect of intersectionality—and in subsequently finding myself dis/connected with a range of continuing feminist debates. Theoretical developments of "intersectionality," arising from feminist conceptualizations, tensions, and struggles over "differences that matter" (Ahmed, 1998) are becoming more sophisticated but such intersectional moves still often neglect a consideration of class and sexuality. In drawing on my research on working-class lesbian lives, I hope to move beyond intersectionality as a theoretical paradigm, toward understanding intersectionality as a lived experience that can be empirically researched and understood, where lives are more than a descriptive list.

CONCLUDING THOUGHTS

Feminist sociologists and geographers have continually struggled with and probed at what the best methodological and theoretical approaches might be in order to cast light on connected categories as they are lived out and contested. Yet not all feminist concerns, dilemmas, and "differences" have entered the debates evenly and equally and this article has attempted to question absences and gaps in feminist research, seeking to hold it up to a higher standard (McCall, 2005). Multiplicity is indeed hard to negotiate but in researching a "hard to reach" group I do not situate intersectionality in the research cohort alone, uncovering an "absence"; rather I see intersectionality within *and* beyond this specific project.

Consideration of the intersections between class and sexuality has, for me at least, given rise to a series of "complexities and complications" about where to situate my research within shifting feminist theoretical frameworks and research agendas. Which women are researched, and the subsequent emergence of theory, is an ongoing feminist dilemma, perhaps intensified in a time of "postmodern questioning," where "old certainties" are given up. I am not seeking to insert class back in as an all encompassing, universal certainty, but rather as a significant intersectional dimension in women's lives. This has been demonstrated through attention to working-class lesbians' varied experiences and identifications, where the interconnected elements of class and sexual inequalities across social spheres, highlight their "real life" effects, beyond the abstract academic page. Like the accounts of Crenshaw (1993) and Berger (2004), I believe that empirically informed accounts of interconnections can foster a more rigorous understanding of women's lives and a more robust research practice and politics of intersectionality.

REFERENCES

Acker, J. "Feminist Theory's Unfinished Business," *Gender and Society*, *22*(1), 2008: 104–108.

Ahmed, S. *Differences that Matter: Feminist Theory and Postmodernism*. Cambridge: Cambridge University Press, 1998.

Anthias, F. and N. Yuval-Davis. "Contextualizing Feminism: Gender, Ethnic and Class Divisions," *Feminist Review*, *15*, 1983: 62–75.

———. "New Hybridities, Old Concepts: The Limits of 'Culture,'" *Ethnic and Racial Studies*, *24*(4), 2001: 619–641.

———. "Beyond Feminism and Multiculturalism: Locating Difference and the Politics of Location," *Women's Studies International Forum*, *25*(3), 2002: 275–286.

Anzaldúa, G. "To(o) Queer the Writer: Loca, Escrito, y Chicana." In C. Trujillo, ed. *Living Chicana Theory*. Berkley, CA: Third Woman Press, 1988.

Berger, M. T. *Workable Sisterhood: The Political Journey of Stigmatized Womanhood with HIV/AIDS*. Princeton, NJ: Princeton University Press, 2004.

———. and K. Guidroz. *The Intersectional Approach*. Chapel Hill: University of North Carolina Press, 2009.

Bradley, H. and G. Hebson. "Breaking the Silence. The Need to Re-Articulate Class," *International Journal of Sociology and Social Policy*, *19*(9), 1999: 178–203.

Brah, A. and A. Phoenix. "Ain't I A Woman? Revisiting Intersectionality," *Journal of International Women's Studies*, *5*(3), 2004: 75–86.

Crenshaw, K. W. "Mapping the Margins: Intersectionality, Identity Politics and Violence Against Women of Color." In A. Albertson Finemanand, R. Mykitiuk, eds. *The Public Nature of Private Violence*. New York: Routledge, 1993: 93–118.

Davis, K. "Intersectionality as Buzzword: A Sociology of Science Perspective on What Makes a Feminist Theory Successful," *Feminist Theory*, *9*(1), 2008: 67–85.

Dunne, G. A. *Lesbian Lifestyles. Women's Work and the Politics of Sexuality*. London: Macmillian Press Limited, 1997.

Epstein, D. *Challenging Lesbian and Gay Inequalities in Education*. Buckingham: Open University Press, 1994.

Giddens, A. *The Transformation of Intimacy: Sexuality, Love and Eroticism in Modern Societies*. Cambridge: Polity Press, 1992.

Hennessey, R. "The Value of a Second Skin." In D. Richardson, J. McLaughlin, and M. Casey, eds. *Intersections in Feminist and Queer Theory.* Basingstoke: Palgrave, 2006: 116–135.

Jackson, S. "Heterosexuality, Sexuality and Gender: Re-thinking the Intersections." In D. Richardson, J. McLaughlin, and M. Casey, eds. *Intersections in Feminist and Queer Theory.* Basingstoke: Palgrave, 2006: 38–58.

Jeffreys, S. *Unpacking Queer Politics: A Lesbian Feminist Perspective.* Oxford: Polity, 2003.

Lutz, H. "Intersectional Analysis: A Way Out of Multiple Dilemmas?" Paper presented at the International Sociological Association conference, Brisbane, July, 2002.

Mac an Ghaill, M. *The Making of Men: Masculinities, Sexualities and Schooling.* Buckingham: Open University Press, 1994.

McCall, L. "The Complexity of Intersectionality," *Signs, 30*(3), 2005: 1771–1800.

McLaughlin, J. "The Return of the Material: Cycles of Theoretical Fashion in Lesbian, Gay and Queer Studies." In D. Richardson, J. McLaughlin, and M. Casey, (eds). *Intersections in Feminist and Queer Theory.* Basingstoke: Palgrave, 2006.

Mizra, H. S., ed. *Black British Feminism: A Reader.* London: Routledge, 1997.

Nayak, A. *Race, Place and Globalization. Youth Cultures in a Changing World.* Oxford: Berg, 2003.

Richardson, D., J. McLaughlin, and M. Casey, eds. *Intersections in Feminist and Queer Theory.* Basingstoke: Palgrave, 2006.

———. and V. Robinson. *Introducing Gender and Women's Studies.* 3rd ed. London: Palgrave, 2007.

Schilt, K. "The Unfinished Business of Sexuality: Comment on Andersen," *Gender and Society, 22*(1), 2008: 109–114.

Skeggs, B. *Formations of Class and Gender.* London: Sage, 1997.

Taylor, Y. "Negotiation and Navigation: An Exploration of the Spaces/Places of Working-Class Lesbians," *Sociological Research Online, 9*(1), 2004: 1–24.

———. "Classed in a Classless Climate," *Feminism and Psychology, 15*(4), 2005: 491–500.

———. *Classed Outsiders: Working-Class Lesbian Life Experiences.* Basingstoke: Palgrave Macmillan, 2007a.

———. "If Your Face Doesn't Fit. . .': The Misrecognition of Working-Class Lesbians in Scene Space," *Leisure Studies, 27*, 2007b: 161–178.

———. "Interesting Intersections? Researching Class, Gender and Sexuality." In M. T. Berger and K. Guidroz, eds. *The Intersectional Approach.* Chapel Hill: University of North Carolina Press, 2009.

Valentine, G. "Out and About: Geographies of lesbian landscapes." *International Journal of Urban and Regional Research* 19(1), 1995: 96–111.

Valentine, G. "Theorizing and Researching Intersectionality: A Challenge for Feminist Geography," *The Professional Geographer, 59*(1), 2007: 10–21.

Weston, K. *Render Me, Gender Me. Lesbians Talk Sex, Class, Color, Studmuffins . . .* New York: Columbia University Press, 1996.

Yuval-Davis, N. "Intersectionality and Feminist Politics." *European Journal of Women's Studies 13*(3), 2006: 193–209.

Researching "Race" in Lesbian Space: A Critical Reflection

NINA HELD

Feminist researchers have acknowledged that racial differences be-tween researcher and researched impact on the research process; however, there has been little concern with how "race" is actually made in/through the research process. If we think "race" as per-formative and as always in the process of being made then this theoretical claim has crucial implications for research encounters. In this article the author draws on her own research, which fo-cuses on processes of racialization. This ethnographic study was conducted in two lesbian bars in the North West of England. The article illustrates different ways of how "race," in particular White-ness, operated during the research process. The author critically reflects on her role in "race making" during this process and high-lights the importance of acknowledging that researchers are also complicit in this making when doing research where "race" is not the central focus.

INTRODUCTION: MAKING "RACE"?

Another of my observation nights. It was a nice mild evening and still light when I was walking down the street heading towards *Jaguars.*[1] The black female bouncer had a quick look into my bag, and after I had heard her "ok," I made my way upstairs to the bar. I opened the door, the room

---

I thank Gail Lewis, Anne-Marie Fortier, and Marjo Kolehmainen for commenting on an earlier draft of this article. Thanks also to the two anonymous reviewers and Lia Kinane for giving useful feedback.

was full with people, sitting on the couches or standing, altogether maybe 200, mostly women but also a few men. There was a lively atmosphere, people standing in groups together and interacting with each other. There were already quite a few people on the dance floor. I hadn't expected such liveliness as it was still quite early for a night out. I sidled between all those bodies moving towards the bar. The bar crew seemed to be in a good mood, all joking and laughing. One of them, a young woman with long blonde hair, tall and slim, wearing a black shirt, black tight trousers and high heels stepped up on the counter and started dancing. Some of the women, and men also, who were standing around, cheered her on hilariously. She persuaded one of the other barmaids to come up to dance with her. A few people in the room joined them in their groove by starting dancing as well. The black barman, who always seems to work, asked me charmingly what I wanted. He then put my drink between the legs of the dancing blonde woman. He also gave me my change back through her legs and smiled at me. I turned around and looked for a place where I could stand. The corner of the bar seemed to offer a good position to do some observations.

To my left a woman was standing who seemed to be on her own as well. She looked a bit miserable. There were three drinks standing in front of her, so presumably she was waiting for two other people. A South Asian woman passed me, she had short dark hair, wore glasses, and was dressed in a white tank top and blue jeans. To my right there was a couple, both probably in their 30s. They both had long hair and wore smart dresses. They looked quite pretty and were clearly very much attracted to each other. A few meters away in front of me I spotted a group of "butch dykes," they all had very short hair and were wearing wide jeans and big T-Shirts. A mixed-race (?) woman came to the bar; she seemed to be excited to meet a woman whose telephone-number she had lost. (Fieldnotes, Saturday, September 23, 2006)

This extract from my research diary describes some of the interactions that took place in a particular sexualized space. Ethnographic writing is always a form of story-telling, and my narrative of what happened in *Jaguars* that night, can only be partial (Clifford, 1986). This narrative is dependant on "how" I *see* and my perception of certain racialized (sexualized, classed) bodies.[2]

Kalpana Seshadri-Crooks (2000) has argued that "race" is a "regime of looking." In the regime that she describes, Whiteness is the "master signifier" and "other" subjects are ascribed racialized positions in relation to it ("Black," "Asian," etc). So while it can be argued that Whiteness seems to work as a silent and unmarked racial category in my fieldnotes, my account also indicates my racialized seeing and my position in this "regime of looking." Critical race theorists have argued that "race" is not a natural/biological category but a social and historical construct. Racial categories are temporally and geographically constructed; the ascribed racial identities can change over time and in different locations (the best example for this is how racial categories have changed in the U.K. Census over the years). "Race" has also been conceptualized as performative and as a social practice through which bodies become continuously racialized in everyday interactions. As Gail Lewis (2007: 873–874) has argued, the "making of race" is a complex process and does not only become apparent through "explicit" racist practices—which are commonly seen as only happening at the edges of (British) society—but in ordinary everyday encounters. That means, as *everybody* is involved in the making of "race," researchers are also complicit in this making (Gunaratnam, 2003).

But how are we actually *making* "race"? Bridget Byrne (2006) argues that "race" is produced through the repetitive use of perceptual practices; that is, how we see or do not see "race" actually produces what we think we see. Drawing on Judith Butler's (1990) concept of performativity she argues that

> 'race' needs to be understood as an embodied performative. That is, that the repeated citation of racialised discourses and, importantly, the repetition of racialised perceptual practices produces bodies and subjects that are raced. What is critical here is that these practices *produce* the idea of differences, rather than being an effect of them. (Byrne 2006: 16, original emphasis)

Butler (1990) argued that the performative repetition of (gendered) norms produces gender. In Byrne's argument it is primarily the repetition of racialized perceptual practices that produces racialized bodies. Thus, according to her theory, "race" is discursively produced through ways of *seeing* difference.

The question now is: How can this theoretical analysis of "race" as performative be used for empirical research? Byrne (2006) herself brought together her theoretical approach with empirical material gained from oral histories with 25 White mothers living in London at the time of the interviews. In her book *White Lives* (2006) she powerfully illustrates her interviewees' perceptual practices and how these practices make "race" in certain ways. However, I would argue that what seems to be needed is that researchers also reflect on their own racialized seeing and on how their perceptual practices might impact on the research process. If "race" is always in process then it is important to look at and reflect on how it is made in/through the research itself. This seems to be even more crucial in ethnographic research where data is produced through everyday interactions and close relationships with the people studied. I want to suggest that Byrne's (2006) approach can be productively employed for issues of reflexivity, which are seen as particularly central in ethnographic research (Davies, 1999: 3; Pink, 2001: 12). In particular, her theory seems to be useful for current methodological discussions on issues of "race making" in ethnographic research (see Alexander,

2006; Gunaratnam, 2003; Twine and Warren, 2000). Participant observations are based on forms of seeing, therefore it is important to be aware of these practices when doing ethnographic research.

In this article I want to illustrate some of the ways "race," in particular Whiteness, operated during the process of my research. I will reflect critically on my own ways of seeing and how my perceptual practices racialized bodies in certain ways during the research process. My participant observations and fieldnotes are based on my own perceptual practices, and if, as Paul Rodaway argues, perception is "a learnt behaviour" (Rodaway, 1994: 11), then part of my seeing of "race" might rely on the way in how I have learnt to see Whiteness as a "neutral" racial category or "non-race." However, as my fieldnotes above might indicate, my perceptions also make sexuality and class in certain ways. Although in this article I will focus on my racialized seeing, I want to urge the reader to think about this seeing as intrinsically sexualized and classed.

"RACE" IN RESEARCH

Feminists have argued that it is important to situate ourselves as researchers, to reflect on our positions, and on how our "partial identities" impact on the research process and the data produced (see, for instance, Haraway, 1988; Harding, 1987). Researchers studying lesbian lives might be aware of the effects of gender and sexuality in the field but is the impact of the researcher's "racial identity" on the research equally considered? One might argue that if "race" is not the focus of research or if we are interviewing lesbians who are from the same ethnic or racial background, then there is no need for reflection on the significance of "race." In fact, some White feminist researchers thought it better to avoid this issue by only including White women in their research samples (for instance, Oakley, 1981, see Edwards, 1990: 483). The effects of samenesses and differences between the interviewer and the interviewee have been highlighted by many feminist researchers (see Bhopal, 2000, 2001; Edwards, 1990; Egharevba, 2001; Fortier, 1998; Johnson-Bailey, 1999). These works show that gender alone is not enough to create "shared meanings" in interviews, as Ann Oakley (1981) had suggested, but that racial, class, and sexual identities play an important role as well.[3]

In the field of "race" and ethnic studies, a few books and edited collections, published by U.S. and British scholars recently, focus on methodological issues when researching "race" (Alexander, 2006; Bulmer and Solomos, 2004; Gunaratnam, 2003; Stanfield and Rutledge, 1993; Twine and Warren, 2000). For instance, Yasmin Gunaratnam (2003) argues in *Researching 'Race' and Ethnicity: Methods, Knowledge and Power* that there is always the risk of reproducing racial categories when researchers use them for analysis. She describes this issue as a "fundamental political and methodological danger" in doing research:

> This danger relates to how categorical approaches can serve to reify 'race' and ethnicity as entities that individuals are born into and inhabit, and that are then brought to life in the social world, rather than 'recognizing' race and ethnicity as dynamic and emergent processes of being and becoming. The conceptual 'fixing' of 'race' and ethnicity is dangerous in terms of the limitations that it can place upon analysis, and because it can serve to produce and reproduce wider forms of essentialism, stereotyping and racism. (Gunaratnam, 2003: 19)

Gunaratnam acknowledges that researching "race" can produce a tension: it is important to acknowledge that racial categories are historically and socially produced as well as constantly in production. But then there is also a need to recognize and grapple with their real life effects such as identity formations, social inequalities, and their materialization in bodies and social relations. Hence, these two different conceptualizations of "race"—as construction and as "real"—can cause dilemma in research.

My research looks at processes of racialization in lesbian spaces. By taking this approach it intends to take into account that "race" is a flexible concept—that it is not fixed but always in process. Nevertheless, my research cannot do without racial categorizations. One of my main research questions, for example, is how the two lesbian bars I am looking at in my research become *White*. Thus, I presume "the pre-existence of 'black' and 'white' as if these were natural and neutrally descriptive terms" (Seshadri-Crooks, 2000: 36).

The use of this categorization manifested itself in my participant observations. At the early stages of my research I was not sure what I should actually "observe" so that I very much focused on what (and how many) "types" of racialized bodies were present in the bars. My racialized seeing worked in this way that I was particularly conscious about the bodies marked as "racially other" and marked out by myself as such. In my fieldnotes I refer to the women and men who I perceived as White just as "women" and "men," and indicate their Whiteness through descriptions of hair for example, while I ascribe "marked" racial identities to a few others. In Byrne's (2006) terms, my perceptual practices made some bodies into "Black," "South Asian," or "mixed-race" bodies while the White bodies were unmarked, not worthy of explicit comment and thus represented the racial norm. Through that I fixed "race" in the way Gunaratnam (2003) describes, whereas the processes of this "race making" remain invisible.

However, I soon realized that it is actually not that easy to "read" somebody's racial identity correctly. In fact, my perceptual practices were often "wrong" by ascribing women racial identities that were not congruent with their self-identification or with the racial group they "officially" belong to (according to Census, etc.).[4] In my fieldnotes Whiteness is produced "simultaneously as a non-racial, 'empty' and yet normative and dominant social location and category of belonging" (Lewis, 2007: 882). My own position in the regime of looking in which Whiteness is the "master signifier" (Seshadri-Crooks, 2000) made it difficult for me to actually see habits of Whiteness. The aim of my participant observations was to find out through which processes the two lesbian spaces become predominantly White and remain White. It was a big challenge for me to change my perceptions, to see the raciality of Whiteness as well and not to leave it in a non-racialized position. It seemed to be impossible to see the construction of Whiteness without bodies racialized as "non-White" being there as well.

This approach also led to other ethical issues, primarily because of the fact that women who can be read as Black or Asian are most of the time easily spotted. That some bodies are usually absent most clearly becomes evident when they are singled out.

> I read Clare's message again which she had sent me just before I left the house. I had told her that I was going out and asked her if she wanted to join me. She texted me that she was tired but that her friend, who I knew is black, was going out, "maybe you'll see her, white shirt, jeans." (Fieldnotes, December 1, 2006)

The two lesbian bars where I did my research are quite popular places, particularly at the weekend, when they attract quite a lot of women. Nevertheless, as Clare's message indicates, the vast majority of these women are readable as White, so that she could assume it would be easy for me to spot her Black friend, although I did not know what she looked like and the description of her clothes would clearly not have distinguished her from many other women there.

My research aimed at gaining accounts from women differently racialized about the racialization of these spaces. The attempt of gaining a "mixed" research sample already relies on racial categories and marks bodies in certain ways, hence it constructs "race." On the other hand, women who are differently racialized, that is, whose bodies are "read" differently are likely to experience these spaces differently because of the real life effects of "race" (Gunaratnam, 2003). I was often tempted to make contact with those women and to ask them what they think about the racialization of these spaces. In fact, one evening in *Jaguars* I approached two Black lesbians with the question as to whether they thought it was "quite White" in there. Of course, this is deeply problematic and furthermore shows that I attached particular meanings to their bodies.

My perceptual practices worked in this way that I defined their racial identity by their skin color and then assumed that because of this physical difference they must be aware of the racialization of these spaces. I also somehow believed that it was important for them to be in "mixed" spaces and that they might feel uncomfortable in "White" spaces. Also in the interviews I was sometimes surprised that ethnic minority women do not necessarily have a critical awareness of "race" issues and racism. Hence, I assumed, as White scholars often do, that ethnic minority people do not "have 'the privilege' to be able to avoid the issue of race" (Twine, 2000: 21).[5]

However, I also had to change my assumptions about White women and that they are unlikely to be conscious of the racialization of the spaces or their Whiteness, as indicated by Byrne's (2006) and Frankenberg's (1993) studies. Furthermore, during my fieldwork I was very conscious about how White women made "race" while it took me longer to see that Black women for instance make "race" as well.

> We are standing next to each other and she encourages me to dance, "move your hips." She tells me that her girlfriend is white but that she has taught her how to dance. (Fieldnotes, August 25, 2006)

Although she is probably right about my dancing, she nevertheless made me into a White woman by attaching the meaning onto my body that White people cannot dance. This also shows that Whiteness is not just invisible but that stereotypes about White people exist (see Hooks, 1997) and that everybody, also "racialized minorities," are involved in processes of racialization (Lewis, 2007).

Furthermore, this example also indicates that it is not only important for researchers to reflect on their own perceptual practices but also on how their bodies are perceived by others in the field, as I will explore in the following.

BEING AND BECOMING WHITE

As I have already argued, "race" is made in everyday interactions, thus, the researcher's body becomes racialized in/through ethnographic encounters. As France Winddance Twine (2000: 17) argues, in certain local and national contexts researchers "frequently have to negotiate the way their bodies are racialised and the meanings attached to these racialisations." Although she refers here to researchers' bodies marked as "racially other" in racially heterogenic fields, also the White researcher's body is racialized even when the field is predominantly White.

The particular racialization of my body made it easy for me to gain entrance to the two lesbian bars as well as other gay bars in the first place, in contrast to some of my participants for whom this was more difficult. As has been outlined by other researchers, lesbians and gay men who are not "read" as being White are more likely to be turned away at the door of

(White) lesbian and gay spaces (GALOP, 2001; Kawale, 2003; Mason-John and Khambatta, 1993).

> It was very busy and we were on the dance floor. When I looked at my mobile, I saw that Chi Li had tried to call me. She had also sent me a text message saying 'They won't let us in. Please come out to gal us up.' First I was wondering how I could help them. I went to the door. I was still inside, they outside and the door man presented a border between us. Chi Li told me that he does not believe that she and Juan were not a heterosexual couple. I tried to negotiate and told him that we were 'regulars.' But he misused his power even more by telling them that they should come back later and that he might let them in then (when it is not as busy). My stomach hurt when I saw her begging him to let them in later and while I was still standing inside I had the strange feeling that my body had more rights to be in that space than theirs. (Fieldnotes, October 6, 2007).

There is some concern that the gay village is becoming increasingly popular for heterosexual customers (see Pritchard et al., 2002). I had heard accounts of White women being questioned inside those spaces about their sexuality because they are perceived to "look heterosexual," whereas only "ethnic minority" women told me about experiences of not being allowed into these spaces in the first place. In particular when the lesbian bars are very busy, the door policies seem to get more exclusive. In Chi Ling's and Juan's case, the bouncer's "gaydar" was definitely wrong (as it quite often is). It might be that their Latin-American and East-Asian identities made it more difficult for him to believe that they were gay, as the "gaydar" is arguably orientated toward certain "White" bodily markers, dress, and habitus. It seemed that I quite fulfill those markers and norms and that my body (and habitus) is easily "read" as lesbian. I had never been refused entrance, had my sexuality questioned, nor was I asked at the door whether I knew what "type" of club it was. I had somehow internalized this "right" to be there such as if it was inscribed on my body. I sometimes confidently led the way, in front of the group, especially when someone was worried about getting in. There were also other occasions where I felt that my White lesbian body and "lesbian habitus" (Rooke, 2005) gave me some advantages in those spaces. I never felt excluded and I never experienced a "look" making me out of place (Held and Leach, 2008). Even at the beginning of my research, when I went to these spaces by myself, I felt quite comfortable. This also because I quite fitted in there; my body did not stand out. One reason for feeling comfortable in those spaces might be that my body was a body "at home" in White space (Ahmed, 2007).

However, from my own position in the field I also realized that perceptual practices not only work visually but through other senses as well. For instance, my body might have been visually marked as White (and maybe British) but when women heard me speaking, it got other attributes attached.[6] I was constantly asked where I was from, followed by discussions about culture and language differences, and it happened a few times that women I just got to know later introduced me to their friends as *the* German. This also indicates that being White cannot be generalized. Whiteness, like any other racial category, is not unitary but part of rather complex processes of racialization. Although my body was "read" as White, I often got marked out in terms of my nationality as revealed by the sound of my voice.[7]

CONCLUSIONS: TO COMPLICATE THE MATTER

This article started from the theoretical premise that "race" is a performative concept, that is, that it is in constant production and that we are *all* involved in its making. The main question leading this article was: How can we translate this theoretical claim into research practice? Byrne's (2006) concept of perceptual practices helped me to reflect on my own racialized seeing and how my perceptions impacted on the research and research encounters. My examples indicated my position in the "regime of looking" in which Whiteness is the "master signifier" (Seshadri-Crooks, 2000). Although my research topic leads to these issues somehow, I hope that my examples of how I "marked" other bodies and how my body was marked, can be useful for other researchers working on different topics as well. Although researching lesbian lives leads to a focus on sexuality, the interconnections with other social categories and how they impact on the research should not be neglected. Furthermore, it needs to be acknowledged that "race" is somehow a feature in every research (Duster, 2000: xii). As long as "race" works as a regime of looking, researchers are always complicit in the making of "race." Although "race making" seems to be impossible to avoid, it is necessary to look at the processes in which it is made and unmade, when it becomes meaning. In this article I have primarily focused on visual perceptual practices and only touched on how hearing also constructs "race." Different senses are mobilized in the re-production of racial differences; bodies are not only racialized through ways of seeing but also through hearing, smelling, and touching. Thus, the next, and even more challenging, step is to reflect on those practices as well when doing research.

NOTES

1. All names used in this article are pseudonyms.
2. My research is based in two lesbian bars in the North West of England. I want to find out how these lesbian spaces get sexualized and racialized, how racialization and sexualization occur, are maintained, and how they get disrupted. I did participant observations and conducted semi-structured interviews with 19 women identifying as White (12); mixed-race (3); Black (3) and Chinese (1). I had met most of the women in these two bars.

3. Edwards (1990) has explored the implications of White women interviewing Black women; Bhopal (2000, 2001) discusses the implications of her South Asian identity for interviewing South Asian women; Johnson-Bailey (1999) the effects of her African-American identity for interviewing African-American women (where class and "color" differences played another role); Egharevba (2001) speaks of experiences of interviewing South Asian women as a Black woman (in which similar experiences with racism had a huge impact); Fortier (1998) describes the complexities of gender, ethnicity, and sexuality in the field.

4. Most often I had mistaken "mixed race" identities for either being White or being Black.

5. However, it was not only me who gave women marked as "racially other" an authentic and authoritative voice during the research process. As Byrne (2006) and Frankenberg (1993) have shown, White women often think that "race" has nothing to do with them. For instance, when I initially presented my research such as "I am looking at the importance of 'race' in lesbian spaces," a typical response from White women was "oh I know a Black lesbian, maybe you can interview her." These women seemed not to consider Whiteness as a racial category nor did they seem to think that they might have anything to say about it in relation to others who are "raced." This leads to Black lesbians being seen as responsible for thinking about the issue. It is then not surprising if they actually do not want to contribute to that kind of research, especially when carried out by a White lesbian researcher, as I had to experience as well (see also Edwards, 1990).

6. For instance, the BBC TV program *What Not to Wear* was once advertised with a comment made by the presenters "Oh My God . . . she looks like a German lesbian" (see McRobbie, 2004: 106). So it seems that there exist some stereotypes about German lesbians that might have an impact on how I might be "read" or perceived.

7. It needs to be said here that the question "Where are You From?" has different implications for others who are actually British but who are marked out visually for not being White (as the nation of the United Kingdom is constructed as White; see Lewis, 2007: 883).

REFERENCES

Ahmed, Sara. "A Phenomenology of Whiteness," *Feminist Theory*, 8(2), 2007: 149–168.

Alexander, Claire. "Introduction: Mapping the Issues," Special Issue "Writing Race: Ethnography and Difference," *Ethnic and Racial Studies*, 29(3), 2006: 397–410.

Bhopal, Kalwant. "Gender, 'Race' and Power in the Research Process: South Asian Women in East London." In Carole Truman, Donna Mertens, and Beth Humphries, eds. *Research and Inequality*. London: UCL Press, 2000: 67–79.

———. "Researching South Asian Women: The Issues of Sameness and Difference in the Research Process," *Journal of Gender Studies*, 10(3), 2001: 279–286.

Bulmer, Martin and John Solomos, eds. *Researching Race and Racism*. London: Routledge, 2004.

Butler, Judith. *Gender Trouble: Feminism and the Subversion of Identity*. London and New York: Routledge, 1990.

Byrne, Bridget. *White Lives: The Interplay of 'Race,' Class and Gender in Everyday Life*. London and New York: Routledge, 2006.

Clifford, James. "Introduction: Partial Truths." In James Clifford, and George Marcus, eds. *Writing Culture: The Poetics and Politics of Ethnography*. Berkeley: University of California Press, 1986: 1–27.

Davies, Charlotte Aull. *Reflexive Ethnography: A Guide to Researching Selves and Others*. London and New York: Routledge, 1999.

Duster, Troy. "Foreword." In France Winddance Twine and Jonathan W. Warren, eds. *Racing Research, Researching Race: Methodological Dilemmas in Critical Race Studies*. New York and London: New York University Press, 2000: xi–xiv.

Edwards, Rosalind. "Connecting Method and Epistemology: A White Woman Interviewing Black Women," *Women's Studies International Forum*, *13*(5), 1990: 477–490.

Egharevba, Itohan. "Researching An-'Other' Minority Ethnic Community: Reflections of a Black Female Researcher on the Intersections of Race, Gender and Other Power Positions on the Research Process," *International Journal of Social Research Methodology*, *4*(3), 2001: 225–241.

Fortier, Anne-Marie. "Gender, Ethnicity and Fieldwork: A Case Study." In Clive Seale, ed. *Researching Society and Culture*. London: Sage, 1998: 48–57.

Frankenberg, Ruth. *White Women, Race Matters: The Social Construction of Whiteness*. London: Routledge, 1993.

GALOP. *The Low Down: Black Lesbians, Gay Men and Bisexual People Talk About Their Experiences and Needs*. London, 2001: http://www.casweb.org/galop/filestorage/view/published_reports/The%20Low%Down, accessed December 20, 2005.

Gunaratnam, Yasmin. *Researching 'Race' and Ethnicity: Methods, Knowledge and Power*. London: Sage, 2003.

Haraway, Donna. "Situated Knowledges: The Science Question in Feminism and the Privilege of Partial Perspective," *Feminist Studies*, *14*, 1988: 575–599.

Held, Nina and Tara Leach. "'What are You Doing Here?': The 'Look' and (non) Belongings of Racialised Bodies in Sexualised Space." In Adi Kuntsman and Esperanza Miyake, eds. *Out of Place: Interrogating Silences in Queerness/Raciality*. York: Raw Nerve Books, 2008: 139–157.

hooks, bell. "Representing Whiteness in the Black Imagination." In Ruth Frankenberg, ed. *Displacing Whiteness: Essays in Social and Cultural Criticism*. Durham and London: Duke University Press, 1997: 165–179.

Johnson-Bailey, Juanita. "The Ties that Bind and the Shackles that Separate: Race, Gender, Class, and Color in a Research Process," *Qualitative Studies in Education*, *12*(6), 1999: 659–670.

Kawale, Rani. "A Kiss is Just a Kiss ... Or is it? South Asian Lesbian and Bisexual Women and the Construction of Space." In N. Puwar and P. Raghuram, eds. *South Asian Women in the Diaspora*. Oxford and New York: Berg, 2003: 181–199.

Lewis, Gail. "Racializing Culture is Ordinary," *Cultural Studies*, *21*(6), 2007: 866–886.

Mason-John, Valerie and Ann Khambatta. *Lesbians Talk Making Black Waves*. London: Scarlet Press, 1993.

McRobbie, Angela. "Notes on 'What Not To Wear' and Post-Feminist Symbolic Violence." In Lisa Adkins and Beverly Skeggs, eds. *Feminism After Bourdieu*. Oxford: Blackwell Publishing, 2004: 97–109.

Oakley, Ann. "Interviewing Women: A Contradiction in Terms." In Helen Roberts, ed. *Doing Feminist Research*. London: Routledge & Kegan Paul, 1981: 30–61.

Pink, Sarah. *Doing Visual Ethnography: Images, Media and Representation in Research*. London: Sage, 2001.

Pritchard, Annette, Nigle Morgan, and Diane Sedgley. "In Search of Lesbian Space? The Experience of Manchester's Gay Village," *Leisure Studies*, *21*, 2002: 105–123.

Rodaway, Paul. *Sensuous Geographies: Body, Sense, Place*. London: Routledge, 1994.

Rooke, Alison Jayne. *Lesbian Landscapes and Portraits: The Sexual Geographies of Everyday Life*. Unpublished thesis: Goldsmiths, London, 2005.

Seshadri-Crooks, Kalpana. *Desiring Whiteness: A Lacanian Analysis of Race*. London and New York: Routledge, 2000.

Stanfield, John and Dennis Rutledge eds. *Race and Ethnicity in Research Methods*. London: Sage, 1993.

Twine, France Winddance and Jonathan W. Warren, eds. *Racing Research, Researching Race: Methodological Dilemmas in Critical Race Studies*. New York and London: New York University Press, 2000.

———. "Racial Ideologies and Racial Methodologies." In France Winddance Twine and Jonathan W. Warren, eds. *Racing Research, Researching Race: Methodological Dilemmas in Critical Race Studies*. New York and London: New York University Press, 2000: 1–34.

Queering Representation:
Ethics and Visibility in Research

RÓISÍN RYAN-FLOOD

This article explores some of the ethical and epistemological dilemmas that arose from a cross-national research project on lesbian motherhood in two European countries, Sweden and Ireland. The differing contexts for sexual citizenship presented particular challenges in relation to negotiating wider norms regarding visibility. Lesbian mothers in Sweden presented a discourse of openness that strongly advocated visibility and the importance of social research in contributing to social change. In contrast to their Swedish counterparts, lesbian mothers in Ireland were more constrained in their efforts to negotiate their claims via visibility and this led to complex choices for the researcher, particularly in relation to contact with popular media.

We do not always seek to make the lives of the oppressed visible to a wide audience. Researching minority lives may have liberatory intent—uncovering the voices of those most often excluded from mainstream narratives—but rendering their lives more visible can have uncomfortable effects. Nast (1994: 60) writes: "For a number of reasons, we do not attempt to make all things apparent to all people." Katz (1994) also suggests that there are potential risks in exposing the lives of the oppressed to the gaze of hegemonic society and dominant groups. What does it mean to uncover the narratives of excluded social groups? Is such unveiling of their lives before an academic or wider audience always positive, for participants and/or researchers? Feminist research writing has long emphasized the importance of producing research that contributes to a wider epistemological project of bringing women's voices in from the margins (Fonow and Cook, 1991; Maynard and Purvis, 1994; Stanley, 1997). Writing that incorporates women's experiences has transformed social research and deconstructed the notion of the unitary universal subject. But it also uncovers a range of ethical, epistemological, and hermeutic questions for the researcher, particularly when doing research on marginalized groups.

Researching lesbian lives can mean uncovering information that may be uncomfortable or impossible to present to a wider audience. It may involve bringing intimate spheres of life to the disciplining gaze of academia and other public realms. These audiences can vary from very supportive to prurient or homophobic. Furthermore, contemporary researchers are often encouraged to engage with audiences beyond the academy. Funding bodies, for example, may require the dissemination of knowledge to "user groups." This can mean presenting the findings to the groups studied or the agencies and institutions they come into contact with. It can also encompass the notion of the "public intellectual" and contributing to a broader public awareness. Questions of visibility, representation, and ethics that arise in this process can create complex dilemmas for the author. In this article, I outline some moments in the research process, writing up, and presentation of results that draw directly on such questions. My experience of carrying out research on lesbian parents in two European countries—Sweden and Ireland—required attention to the complexities of researching, writing, and presenting material on a particular minority group. This included decisions about whether or not to engage with the media, and keeping a low profile for the research project while simultaneously trying to recruit a wide sample of participants.

SEXUAL CITIZENSHIP IN A COMPARATIVE PERSPECTIVE

The two countries provide an intriguing contrast for approaches to sexual citizenship. On the surface, it might appear that Sweden is far more progressive in relation to sexual equality and this is broadly speaking a fair assessment. Yet if you scratch beneath the surface, a more complex picture emerges. Sweden was one of the first countries to introduce legal recognition for same-sex relationships in the form of registered partnerships in 1995. However, the same legislation explicitly prohibited all parenting possibilities, including adoption and access to new reproductive technologies. Subsequently this became the key terrain for lesbian, gay, bisexual, and transgender (LGBT) equality struggles and at the time I began carrying out fieldwork in 2000, it was a high-profile policy issue. The laws have since been changed to allow same-sex couples to adopt and access assisted reproduction, although some inequalities remain.

Ireland does not currently offer any legal recognition to same-sex partnerships. Interestingly, however, lesbian and gay parenthood have been relatively unregulated compared to Sweden. There is no law expressly prohibiting lesbians from access to assisted conception, although in practice it remains difficult for them to do so. Health boards have also advertised for foster parents in lesbian and gay publications. This is not, however, because they are hugely supportive of LGBT parents. Rather, there is such a shortage of foster parents that they have had to develop more inclusive criteria.

I carried out interviews with 68 lesbians parents in the two countries. All participants embarked on parenthood in the context of an openly lesbian lifestyle. Although it is the case that lesbians have always been parents, previous generations of lesbian women typically became parents in the context of a heterosexual relationship, coming out later in life. A new generation of lesbian women are becoming parents after coming out. This study explored the subjectivities, family practices, and processes of citizenship among this group in two European countries.

SWEDEN—DISCOURSE OF OPENNESS

Upon arrival in Sweden, I was immediately struck by the degree to which lesbian and gay parenting was a topic of debate. Swedish media and political discussion have devoted considerable attention to "homosexual families" in recent years. The level of public discussion about lesbian and gay parenting was particularly intense during the period of fieldwork, with calls for more research in the area from numerous sources, including the Swedish government. I found the LGBT organizations I made contact with very helpful. Their encouragement was perhaps based on the conviction that more awareness based on research could only be beneficial in the struggle for equal rights. Overall, it was relatively easy to make contact with participants in Sweden. Throughout my experience of research there, I have encountered a general support for academic research and willingness to participate among people working in a variety of sectors (Ryan-Flood, 1998, 2009a). This is possibly because of a more dynamic interaction between academia and public life in Sweden than I have observed in the United Kingdom and Ireland. Furthermore, the political potential of the research often seemed to play a role in participants' decisions to take part. During conversations before and after interviews, I frequently got the impression that interviewees viewed their participation in the research project as the responsibility or gesture of a "good citizen," in that it was seen as a social contribution that would benefit the wider community. As McDowell (1999) notes, researchers may inadvertently raise participants' expectations that research will constitute a positive intervention on their behalf. However, Swedish participants appeared confident of the benefits of research, in the absence of any such promises on my part.

Andreasson (1996) argues that "openness" has displaced "resistance" as a normative signifier of a political strategy in contemporary Swedish LGBT politics. According to his analysis, this is reflected in the increasing number of openly lesbian and gay people in Swedish mass media. Openness has therefore become the predominant means by which lesbian and gay people assert and defend their sexual identity in Sweden. As Foucault (1978) argued, discourses of sexuality change over time and according to context. Thus, what I term a "discourse of openness" appears to be predominant among lesbian parents in contemporary Sweden. This discourse of openness was apparent during interviews with Swedish participants, who frequently referred to the importance of "openness" about their family forms. It was seen as necessary to be open about their sexuality for the sake of their children. Refusing to pass as heterosexual was also perceived as a means of challenging prejudice:

> We made a decision when we were waiting for [expecting] Jacob [eldest child] that all four of us should be very open, that we should be very open in every place where our kids were, not a secret and of course you don't say when you meet somebody hi I'm Hanna and I'm a lesbian, you don't do it like that but in every situation that somebody asks or me or you or Olof or Johan [gay fathers] something we don't deny anything [. . .] and then we are very open everywhere else [. . .] because we are so open and we make these demands I think we help others.
>
> —Hanna, Swedish participant parenting with her partner and a gay couple

Hanna's sexuality, and that of the other three people she shared parenting responsibilities with, was not an "open secret"; rather, it was something that was clearly communicated, although in ways sensitive to the immediate context. It was important to establish that Hanna and her partner are a lesbian couple and that the two men they parent with are a gay couple. The possibility of their sexuality being unclear or unacknowledged was unacceptable. This discourse of openness was very striking in the Swedish sample. Although Irish parents also shared their conviction that it was important to be open for their children's sake, they were likely to do it in a less overt or confrontational way. In Ireland, for example, the role of both partners in a couple relationship as parents was communicated, but in a way that emphasized their status as parents or guardians, rather than their sexuality as a lesbian couple. In both contexts, participants emphasized the importance of being "open" about their family form for the sake of their children. However, Irish participants communicated this information in a more indirect way. This contrast illustrates some of the central differences between Swedish and Irish participants in my study with regard to what it means to be "out" as a lesbian parent. These distinctions have informed ethical considerations regarding the potential impact of this research.

NEGOTIATING (IN)VISIBILITY IN IRELAND

Lesbian and gay activism in Ireland has been influenced by nationalist politics and postcolonial identities. The concept of an indigenous lesbian and gay politics therefore holds particular significance among Irish activists (Rose, 1994; Bowyer, 2001). Thus, confrontational models of queer activism are often viewed as a cultural import and therefore problematic. Nonetheless, increased lesbian and gay visibility and established events such as annual Pride in Irish cities have been utilized by Irish LGBT communities in the struggle for equality. Although considerable advances have been made in recent years and research indicates growing levels of acceptance, especially among young people (Inglis, 1998), homophobia remains widespread.

After embarking on fieldwork in Ireland, I soon observed the contrast with Sweden in terms of the very different levels of media and political debate about queer parenting. I became aware of what seemed to me a deafening silence regarding lesbian parenting, particularly embarking on the Irish fieldwork immediately after leaving Sweden, where it was a source of intense discussion. This is not to undermine the greater prominence given to lesbian and gay issues in contemporary Irish media, where they have a much higher profile than in previous decades. However, it was illustrative of the different political moments in both countries and the politicized meanings of visibility for participants. In contrast to Swedish participants, for whom "speaking out" about their families constituted an important political gesture, Irish participants tended to live out their lesbian identities in a more segregated way.

Although participants who volunteered for my research clearly believed that it was important to tell their stories, the impact of the media occasionally arose during interviews. Sorcha, an Irish lesbian mother, described her experience during late pregnancy when chatting with a woman she met in the park. They had both seen a documentary about lesbian and gay parenting that had been aired on the BBC. Despite this, the woman she spoke with assumed that her obvious pregnancy implied Sorcha was heterosexual and commented negatively about the program, which Sorcha found very distressing:

> There was one that I encountered while I was pregnant remember, that was awful, it was just, just awful [...] so I'm walking around with my big baby and my impending motherhood and all of a sudden this thing came back to me, it was following a programme that was on the tv, you might have seen it, it was on BBC2 [...] and it was called pink parents [...] We saw that and it was great you know [...] and it came about when I met a stranger you know that I had seen this thing [...] and she said to me obviously never having laid eyes on me before in her life, oh you saw that as well, it was scary wasn't it? And that's the first time in a long time

that I had experienced that kind of like direct, direct thing that people out there actually think, think it's scary the thought of us being parents, is actually scary to them and I thought Jesus Christ you know.

—Sorcha, Irish participant

In this example, a key factor is Sorcha's presumed heterosexuality. However, the incident is illustrative of the way that public discussion can have painful repercussions for individuals whose lifestyle is the topic of debate. However, although upset because of the response from the woman she met in the park, Sorcha expressed delight with the program itself and her own experience of watching it.

Nonetheless, the potentially negative impact for participants of greater awareness about lesbian parenting was also made apparent when another participant, Catherine, talked about her reaction to a radio program where the subject of lesbian and gay parenting arose:

Every time that the topic comes up on the radio like the Gerry Ryan show[1] or whatever [. . .] and every time that kind of stuff comes up I have to deal with the repercussions because I'm an out lesbian. I'll walk down the street and every single person has to have a comment about that then to me, whether or not I want to hear it or discuss it you know. Every single person will have something to comment you know, you're actively having to deal with that all the time. It was a bit of the thing of whether or not you know, how you actually do use publicity and everything, how you, what effect having somebody on the television or on the radio has on other people you know and how you actually take responsibility for that.

—Catherine, Irish participant

Catherine's comments reflect the dilemma of equality struggles in an Irish context. On the one hand, it appears that the lesbian and gay movement must advocate parenting rights and challenge prejudice by drawing attention to the issue and refuting homophobic assumptions about queer parenting. On the other hand, to do so may make life difficult for lesbian and gay parents in the short term, who become more vulnerable to verbal and other abuse. I wrote an article about lesbian and gay parenting for *Gay Community News*, a monthly Irish publication, partly as a means of recruiting participants for my research (Ryan-Flood, 2001). However, this was written for a national lesbian and gay publication and therefore a sympathetic audience. Another Irish researcher provided some comments about lesbian parenting for a radio show about families in Ireland. Prior to her appearance on the show, we discussed the ethical difficulties involved in contributing to media discussion. At that stage of the research, I decided that I would not feel comfortable contributing as I was unsure whether I would ever want to discuss my research findings outside of queer venues and sympathetic (gender/women's/queer studies) academic audiences in Ireland. This researcher was interviewed for the program and provided an excellent foil to some of the homophobic comments/assumptions that were discussed. Nonetheless, afterwards she confessed to me that she felt relieved that it was a small slot on a low ratings show and therefore unlikely to receive much attention. I have also been approached by researchers within the media in Ireland. In one case, I agreed to have my contact details forwarded to staff of an Irish television program, who were considering doing a piece on lesbians and reproduction (inspired by discussions of the "mannotincluded" online sperm facility in the United Kingdom at the time). However, I stipulated that I would be involved in a consultancy role only. The decision about whether to agree to be considered as an academic consultant was not an easy one. Finally I decided that if I agreed to contribute in this role, I could perhaps help to ensure that a supportive perspective was communicated.

In retrospect, it is interesting to note that while in Ireland I engaged in many of the same practices in negotiating (in)visibility as the Irish participants in this study. When attempting to elicit relevant information from various authorities, or deciding how open (or not) to be about my research to various audiences, I often deployed a strategy of indirect enquiry/communication, similar to that exercised by many participants in negotiating their daily lives. For example, I phoned individual fertility clinics in Ireland in an effort to find out if they offered their services to lesbians. Enquiring about whether services are available to lesbian women may provoke an explicit policy being implemented, where previously women might have benefited from the lack of specific guidelines concerning clients' sexuality. I realized that if a clinic provided services to heterosexual single women and I asked specifically about lesbian women, this could potentially alert them to the fact that lesbians might be interested in donor insemination (DI). The clinic could then become inclined to devise a policy specifically prohibiting lesbians from accessing the clinic, whereas having no specific policy on this might be beneficial to lesbian women. Alternatively, it might alert them to the possibility that theoretically lesbians can pose as single heterosexual women to use their services, if a clinic is willing to accept single women as clients. So I chose to ask indirectly and find out what kinds of criteria clients had to fulfill.

It appeared that no clinic was willing to state explicitly that it would treat clients who were not in a heterosexual relationship. Previously, the Well Woman clinic in Dublin had openly advertised its services to all women, including lesbians. However, that particular clinic decided to terminate its sperm bank in 1999 due to financial difficulties and referred enquiries to a private clinic in Dublin. I rang the private clinic and was informed that they treat heterosexual couples only. They referred me to another clinic in Belfast. That clinic also stated that they only accept heterosexual couples. Further enquiries at various clinics around the country received the same response.

There is no specific legislation prohibiting lesbians from access to sperm banks, although medical council guidelines do state that this service should only be used in cases of infertility and genetic problems. Nonetheless, at this time it appears that no clinic in Ireland was willing to openly admit that it would offer this service to lesbians.

ENGAGING WITH THE MEDIA: IMPLICATIONS FOR RESEARCHERS

So far I have outlined some of the pressures on researchers in negotiating representation and the research process. These include: a concern with preventing harmful outcomes for participants; and navigating complex cultural contexts in relation to strategies of openness and visibility utilized by participants.[2] Further dilemmas arise when thinking of the personal consequences for researchers who write about intimate life. Although sexualities has become a well-established field of academic work, this is not to say that it is without professional and personal risks for researchers. Attwood (2009), for example, discusses the complexities of researching pornography, which can elicit scornful, amused, and uncomfortable responses from colleagues, or hostility. Moving the realm of engagement beyond academia also presents particular challenges.

Contemporary culture is saturated with images of sexuality. Sex is used to sell everything from coffee to cars. Indeed, this contemporary "preoccupation with sexual values, practices and identities" is referred to as the "sexualization of culture" (Attwood, 2006: 77). Plummer (1995) argues that a new culture of "telling sexual stories" has emerged, in which people are more open about narratives of sexual and intimate life. This enables them both to process their experiences, and also to establish intimacy. So a particular regime of sexual life in the public realm has developed. The media produces avid reports of both everyday and outlandish sexual stories. For researchers of sexuality and intimate life, any engagement with the media is tempered by an awareness that bringing research findings and stories to the public realm opens up the possibility of our work being distorted in sensationalist ways. The rise in reflexivity in academic work, where researchers situate themselves in relation to their own identity, allows for greater transparency in the research process and develops the epistemological terrain, exploring how researcher and participant dynamics informs the empirical material. However, this openness both within and beyond the Academy can make the researcher potentially vulnerable.

Valentine's (1998) classic article provides a spatial analysis of her experience as the victim of a campaign of homophobic harassment that took place largely in her academic workplace but also involved the perpetrator outing her to her immediate family. Her analysis illustrates how work and home spaces constitute crucial spaces in the construction of a "safe" identity. Dunne (2004) discusses the way in which her work on the division of labor among lesbian parents became sensationalized and distorted within the media. Her argument that lesbian couples can develop creative new ways of managing the division of household labor that are conducive to equality was presented as an argument that "lesbians can make better parents" (in Hallowell et al., 2004). Another researcher in the United Kingdom who gave a presentation on research into polyamory at a national conference found her work distorted and sensationalized by the press. In her presentation she acknowledged that she was a member of the communities that she researched—bisexual and polyamorous. She also referred to the book *The Ethical Slut* by Easton and Liszt (1997), a key text in work on polyamory. A national newspaper subsequently ran a story with the headline "Bisexual Boffin: I'm a Slut" accompanied by her name and photograph.[3] The Danish researcher Dag Heede experienced public controversy over his attempts to "queer" readings of the biography of national icon Hans Christian Andersen. Furthermore, in encounters with the media, as an openly gay academic he was treated differently compared to his heterosexual counterparts. Thus, he was invited to pose semi-dressed for interview photographs. One interviewer requested that he pose wearing only his pajama bottoms on top of his unmade bed. He declined. This suggests that the intellectual value of academic work can be trivialized in cases where media attempt to sexualize the researcher. The personal repercussions of such encounters for individual researchers can be highly distressing. In attendance at training workshops in dealing with the media, I have been informed that an interest in the personal identities of the researcher on the part of the media is perhaps to be expected. However, we must simultaneously recognize that this may open the researcher up to profoundly uncomfortable, or indeed oppressive, experiences. The consequences for the researcher can include both personal attacks or an undermining of their work in more subtle ways. This may include the implication that a lesbian who writes about lesbians, for example, has a biased perspective. The assumption of bias relates to the traditional positivist emphasis on objectivity and the presumed neutrality of the researcher. Of course, a heterosexual researcher writing about lesbian and gay communities would be less likely to face this accusation and instead be considered an impartial observer.

My research on lesbian parenthood resulted in some unexpected findings. An exploration of discourses of fatherhood among lesbian parents, for example, revealed that although lesbian parents in both countries had a preference for a known donor, Swedish lesbians were far more likely to choose donors who played an active parenting role. In contrast, Irish lesbians liked to know who the donor was, but for that information to remain confidential. He would typically have no contact with the child or any caretaking or financial responsibilities. The option was open, however, for the child to contact him when they were older if they expressed curiosity about him. These striking differences were a reflection of wider cultural constructions of gender, families, and reproductive choice. I have written elsewhere about the implications of these findings for theories of gender, kinship, and citizenship (Ryan-Flood, 2005a, 2005b, 2009a). When approached by media in Ireland about my research toward the end of fieldwork, I was conscious of how these sensitive findings could be misinterpreted and distorted. At the time, there was considerable discussion of "the rights of fathers" in Ireland, echoing a "families need fathers" rhetoric. The social climate did not seem particularly conducive to a sympathetic reading of my work. I decided that it would be best to wait until my findings had been published in academic journals and books. Once the work is an academic publication, it is perhaps easier to defend and clarify in that there is a written record of your arguments and interpretations, rather than interview soundbites. Although it may be the case that my research findings would have evoked little or no response from groups unsupportive of families that do not fit into a traditional heteronormative model, in my view it would have been unethical not to consider the potential repercussions of this research for participants. Furthermore, the concerns that are outlined here are of relevance to broader discussions regarding social research ethics and epistemology.

CONCLUSION: UNEASY RESOLUTIONS

This article has addressed some ethical dilemmas encountered in the research process. In particular, the tension between the need to tell women's stories and negotiate their vulnerability in homophobic contexts has been a point of analysis. The impact of strategies of openness and invisibility have been discussed in terms of their epistemological implications during the recruitment of participants and the process of data collection and analysis. Participant confidentiality and anonymity remain central to the presentation of data. The ethical dilemmas encountered challenge conceptualizations of "the field" as a spatially bounded entity. Rather, it is the nature of political standpoints and community belonging that relationships and events influencing "the field" continue to evolve long after a period spent in a particular geographical location is concluded. By thus politically situating "the field," it becomes clear why issues of representation and ethics have been so central to the research process (Nast, 1994).

The dilemma of openness and representation has also been addressed in terms of the consequences of researchers' engagement with the "public worlds" of the academy and discursive terrain of the media. It is not the intention of this author to conflate these two spheres, but rather to highlight the ways in which they may potentially overlap in terms of participants' vulnerability. Further, work automatically becomes available to diverse users once it is disseminated within the public arena of the academy. The two national contexts of the research highlight the different ways that participants may hope research will be utilized and thus varied understandings of the role of visibility in multiple terrains, including the academy and the media. It is also illustrative of the dialogical nature of research, in which participants are not passive objects but agentic subjects.

Although it is hoped that a study may have a positive impact on participants' lives by informing the policy-making process, this research is characterized by a continual negotiation of the potentially negative consequences of rendering aspects of these women's lives visible to a public domain. However, research about lesbian parenting in contemporary Irish and Swedish society that is both sympathetic and rigorous does not in itself "cause" homophobia. Although I remain concerned about the possibility of certain groups distorting my work, a moratorium on research about this topic because of homophobia is not, in my view, an acceptable alternative. Censorship of this kind is not always an appropriate solution and may constitute another victory for those hostile to families that do not adhere to a heteronormative form. My uneasy resolution of this difficult issue therefore has been to continue with this research and to write about the findings. I retain a strong commitment to dissemination of the research findings among user groups such as the LGBT community and policy-makers. However, even if a researcher faces the possibility that public debate may be intensified in negative ways as a result in the short-term, the need for discursive interventions that are sympathetic to lesbian and gay subjects in order to counter widespread homophobia remains. Furthermore, it has become apparent that a strategy of relative invisibility will not be possible indefinitely. Since the completion of my research study, there has been greater discussion of lesbian and gay parenting in Ireland than ever before, largely influenced by events in the rest of Europe with regard to legislative changes concerning LGBT equality. It likely that this debate will continue to expand. This research therefore hopefully constitutes a contribution to the undermining of hegemonic heteronormative discourses.

NOTES

1. A popular radio show in Ireland.

2. I have written elsewhere about dilemmas of secrecy and silence in the research process, including my choice not to disclose information about illegal activities undertaken by participants when writing up research (Ryan-Flood, 2009b).

3. See Barker (2006) for further discussion of the consequences of being out in academia.

REFERENCES

Andreasson, M. *Öppenhet och Motstånd: Om homosexualitet i massmedia 1990–1994* [Openness and Resistance: On Homosexuality in the Massmedia 1990–1994]. Stockholm: Folkhälsoinstitutet, 1996.

Attwood, F. "Sexed Up: Theorizing the Sexualization of Culture," *Sexualities*, 9(1), 2006: 77–94.

———. "Dirty Work: Researching Women and Sexual Representation." In R. Ryan-Flood and R. Gill, eds. *Secrecy and Silence in the Research Process: Feminist Reflections*. London: Routledge, 2009: (forthcoming).

Barker, M. "Sexual Self-Disclosure and Outness in Academia and the Clinic," *Lesbian & Gay Psychology Review*, 7(3), 2006: 292–296.

Bowyer, S. "Coming Out to the Neighbourhood/Coming On to the Neighbours: Same Sex Desire, Speaking it and Being it in Dublin 2001." *Paper for presentation at the 3rd IASSCS, October 1–3, 2001*.

Dunne, G. A. "The Lion, the Witch and the Wardrobe: Reflections on Interviewing Men." In S. Gregory, N. Hallowell, and J. Lawton, eds. *Reflection on Research: The Research Methods Book With A Difference*. Open University Press 2004.

Easton, D. and C. A. Liszt. *The Ethical Slut: A Guide to Infinite Sexual Possibilities*. California: Greenery Press, 1997.

Fonow, M. and J. A. Cook, eds. *Beyond Methodology: Feminist Scholarship as Lived Research*. Bloomington: Indiana University Press, 1991.

Foucault, M. *The History of Sexuality, Volume 1: The Will to Knowledge*, Harmondsworth: Penguin Books, 1978, 1990.

Hallowell, N., J. Lawton, and S. Gregory. *Reflections on Research: The Realities of Doing Research in the Social Sciences*. Milton Keynes: Open University Press, 2004.

Heede, D. "Notes on a Scandal: Reflections on Queering a National Icon." In R. Gill and R. Ryan-Flood, eds. "Special Feature—Secrecy and Silence in the Research Process: Feminist Reflections," *Feminism and Psychology*, 18(3), 2008: 410–416.

Inglis, T. *Lessons in Irish Sexuality*. Dublin: University College Dublin Press, 1998.

Katz, C. "Playing the Field: Questions of Fieldwork in Geography," *Professional Geographer*, 46(1), 1994: 67–72.

Maynard, M. and J. Purvis. *Researching Women's Lives from a Feminist Perspective*. London: Taylor & Francis, 1994.

McDowell, L. *Gender, Identity and Place: Understanding Feminist Geographies*. Oxford: Polity Press, 1999.

Nast, H. "Opening Remarks on 'Women in the Field,'" *Professional Geographer*, 46(1), 1994: 54–66.

Plummer, K. *Telling Sexual Stories: Power, Change and Social Worlds*. London: Routledge, 1995.

Rose, K. *Diverse Communities: The Evolution of Lesbian and Gay Politics in Ireland*. Cork: Cork University Press, 1994.

Ryan-Flood, R. "The Rape Crisis Services in Dublin and Stockholm— A Comparative Study," M.Phil. dissertation in Women's Studies, Trinity College, Dublin, 1998.

———. "Contested Heteronormativities: Discourses of Fatherhood Among Lesbian Parents in Sweden and Ireland," *Sexualities*, 8(2), 2005a: 189–204.

———. "Lesbiskt föraldraskap i Sverige och på Irland." In D. Kulick, ed. *Queer Sverige*. Stockholm: Natur och Kulture, 2005b.

———. *Lesbian Motherhood: Gender, Families and Sexual Citizenship*. Basingstoke: Palgrave-MacMillan, 2009a.

———. "Keeping Mum: Secrecy and Silence in Research on Lesbian Parenthood." In R. Ryan-Flood and R. Gill, eds. *Secrecy and Silence in the Research Process: Feminist Reflections.* London: Routledge, 2009b: (forthcoming).

Stanley, L. *Knowing Feminisms.* London: Sage, 1997.

Valentine, G. "Sticks and Stones May Break My Bones: A Personal Geography of Harassment," *Antipode, 30,* 1998: 303–332.

Index

Note: Page numbers followed by "n" denote endnotes.

abuse 4, 47, 48, 50, 53–56, 105
abusive behaviors 4, 48, 50, 51, 53–56
Akass, K. 60
Andreasson, M. 103
Anthias, F. 79
Anzaldúa, G. 77
Attwood, F. 107

Babb, Florence E. 24
Badgett, M. V. Lee 23
Bauman, Z. 13
Beck, U. 67
Bennett, Judith M. 31n4
Berger, M. T. 79, 86
Billig, M. 15, 19n5
bisexual women 3, 35
Black lesbian 93, 97n5
Bourdieu, P. 37
Bradley, H. 78
Butler, J. 90
Byrne, Bridget 90, 92, 94, 96, 97n5

Chambers, S. 60
children 52, 53, 56, 103
class 5, 17, 24, 65, 66, 75, 76, 78–82,
    84–86, 91
complexities 4, 5, 18, 24, 36, 42, 74,
    76–78, 81, 101, 107
complications 5, 25, 74, 85
consumer-citizen 61, 65
cosmopolitan girls 65
cosmopolitan sexual citizens 4, 59, 70
Cossman, B. 62, 69
Crenshaw, K. W. 79
cultural citizenship 63, 65
culture, sexualization of 107

Davies, C. 68
domestic abuse 47, 51, 52, 55
domestic violence 4, 46–53, 56; experiences of
    4, 55, 56; impact of 49
Dunne, G. A. 84, 107

Easton, D. 108
Edwards, Rosalind 97n3
Egharevba, Itohan 97n3
emotions 3, 9, 34, 36–39, 82, 84
erotic subjectivity 38
ethical dilemmas 6, 41, 109
ethics 4, 6, 35–37, 51, 52, 100, 101, 109
ethnicity 48, 49, 52, 80, 91, 92
ethnographers 35, 37–39
ethnographic field ork 3, 5, 34
ethnographic research 3–5, 35, 38, 90, 91
ethnographic self 4, 35, 42
ethnography 3, 4, 34, 35, 38, 42
Evans, D. T. 68
exclusions 29, 41, 74, 76, 77

female agency 12
feminist epistemological approach 4, 46, 48
feminist scholarship 47
first same-sex relationship 53, 5
flexibility 3, 13, 14, 16–1
flexible selfhood 1
Fortier, Anne-Marie 97n3
Foucault, M. 103
Frankenberg, Ruth 94, 97n5

gay 3, 4, 15, 16, 23, 24, 38, 47–50, 53, 54, 56, 62;
    parenting 102, 104, 105, 110; women 53, 54
Geertz, Clifford 32n8
gender 4, 5, 17, 48, 49, 52, 53, 56, 69, 75, 76, 78, 79,
    91, 109; categories of 15, 17
Gunaratnam, Yasmin 91, 92

Halberstam, J. 68
Hart, L. 70n4
Hebson, G. 78
Hemmings, C. 19n2
heteroflexible 3, 1
hetero/lesbian 11, 12, 14, 15, 18
"heteronormative" demographics 52–54
heterosexuality 2, 10, 12, 17, 62, 68, 69
heterosexualization 10, 11

heterosexual relationships 4, 11, 46–51, 102, 106
heterosexual women 47, 49, 77
homosexuality 17, 22, 23

inclusion 14, 23, 27, 29, 40, 69, 75, 76
informants 4–6, 37–39, 42
intersectional case study 80
intersectional methodologies 79
intersectional re-runs 76, 77
intersections/intersectionality 2, 4–5, 48, 74–81,
   84–86
(in)visibility 104, 106
Ireland 6, 22, 101–107, 109, 110
Island, D. 48

Johnson-Bailey, Juanita 97n3

Katz, C. 100
kinship 31, 109

Laing, R. D. 17
lesbian: bars 5, 92–95; chic 11, 12, 14, 16; couple 69,
   103, 108; identities 11, 26, 28, 39–42, 104; life 66;
   parenting 104, 105, 110; parents 6, 101–103, 108;
   relationships 4, 28, 47, 48, 50, 55, 56; sexualities 8,
   17, 61; space 5, 80, 83, 88, 92, 93; subjectivities 5,
   61, 69, 70; visibility 11
lesbianism 11, 15, 16
Letellier, P. 48
Lewis, Gail 90
Liszt, C. A. 108
Luibheid, Eithne 29
Lury, C. 18
Lutz, H. 78

male relationships 47, 51, 54
Marcus, George E. 32n8
margins, mapping 79
Martin, E. 13
masculinity 47, 68, 69
McCabe, J. 60
McCall, L. 76, 80
McCarthy, A. 63, 64
McDowell, L. 102
media 6, 62, 101, 104, 106–110
Mort, F. 10

Nast, H. 100
neo-liberalism 4, 5, 12, 13, 17, 18
neoliberal politics 65
Nixon, S. 10

Oakley, A. 91
openness 6, 16, 84, 102, 103, 107, 109; discourse of
   102, 103

Panourgiá, Neni 32n8
perceptual practices 90–96

performativity 3, 4, 34, 35, 39, 40, 90
Plummer, K. 10, 107
psychopathology 10, 14, 17, 18

queer 23, 25, 34, 36, 38, 41, 42, 50, 53, 60, 62–65, 77;
   ethnographer 36; ethnography 4, 35, 42; subjects
   3, 8, 62; theory 2, 39, 40, 77
Queer Eye 62–64
queering representation 6, 100

racial/race 5, 17, 48, 49, 75, 78, 79, 88–94,
   96; categories 5, 79, 89–93, 96; differences 67,
   69, 96
Ramazanoğlu, C. 50
realities 48, 49, 61, 81
Renzetti, C. M. 48
representation 2–6, 8–12, 14, 15, 35, 60, 109
representational practices 9, 17, 18
research process 5, 6, 39–41, 90, 91, 101, 107, 109
Ristock, J. 48, 55
Rosaldo, Renato 28

same-sex 4, 47, 48, 64; relationships 4, 26, 46–48, 50,
   51, 53–55, 62
scene spaces 80, 83, 84
self 14, 27, 28, 35, 36, 39, 42, 62, 63, 66
self-identification 25–27, 93
Seshadri-Crooks, Kalpana 89
sexuality 2, 5, 10, 11, 17, 18, 28, 31, 40, 48, 49, 52–54,
   56, 75, 78, 85, 103, 107
sexual/sex 12, 15, 17, 26, 40, 50, 54, 56, 61, 107;
   abuse 55, 56; citizens 61, 62, 64–67, 70; citizenship
   4, 6, 61, 62, 70, 101; difference 18, 69
sexual subjectivity 38, 39, 42
Skeggs, B. 17
spaces 39–42, 49, 76, 83, 93–95, 107
Stein, Arlene 28
subjectivities 2, 3, 6, 9, 10, 12, 14, 18, 41, 102
Sweden 6, 101–104

temporality 3, 34, 42
Twine, France Winddance 94

Valentine, G. 80, 107
Vance, C. 12
visibility 104

Walker, Lisa 29
Whiteness 80, 89, 91–94, 96
White women 91, 94, 95
White working-class lesbian 37
women 12, 15, 16, 25, 26, 40, 41, 49, 53, 54, 65, 76,
   77, 79, 80, 85, 86, 89, 92, 93, 96, 104–106; lesbian
   relationship 69
working class 5, 41, 81; lesbians 3, 34, 67, 75, 76, 80,
   82–86

Yuval-Davis, N. 78